Merry Christmas
Noel!

P 2007

Digby Law's

SOUP

COOKBOOK

A New Zealand classic

Books by Digby Law

Digby Law's
SOUP
COOKBOOK

A New Zealand classic

Hodder Moa

A catalogue record for this book is available from the National Library of New Zealand.

ISBN: 978-1-86971-103-0

Originally published in 1982 by Hodder & Stoughton

A Hodder Moa Book
Published in 2007 by Hachette Livre NZ Ltd
4 Whetu Place, Mairangi Bay
Auckland, New Zealand

Designed and produced by Hachette Livre NZ Ltd
Printed by Griffin Press, Australia

Front cover: Carrot and Lemon Soup, page 73

Contents

Digby Law

1936–1987

Digby Law was a gourmet chef, food writer and broadcaster whose cookery books helped change the way New Zealanders approach food and eating. He was a pioneer of New Zealand food, taking what grew in our gardens and suggesting new ways of cooking and eating it. His positive encouragement led many cooks to a true appreciation of ingredients and flavours.

On his death in 1987, his first series of cookbooks had sold in excess of 100,000 copies and still remain in constant demand.

INTRODUCTION

Beautiful soup! Who cares for fish
Game, or any other dish?
Who would not give all else for two
Pennyworth only of beautiful soup?
Lewis Carroll, *Alice's Adventures in Wonderland*

What is soup?

The dictionaries all define soup as 'a liquid food'. Webster continues: 'having as a base meat, fish, or vegetable stock being clear or thickened to the consistency of a thin purée, or having milk or cream added and often containing pieces of solid food (as meat, shellfish, pasta or vegetables).' Collins elaborates: 'prepared by boiling, usually consisting of an extract of meat with other ingredients and seasoning.'

But there is much more to soup than that. Shall we say that soup is a liquid food made out of anything edible. The word comes from the Latin 'suppa' as does the word 'supper' which originally consisted of soup.

Soup has been described as being 'to a dinner what a portico is to a house'. It should announce the full tones of the meal 'as an overture of an opera announces the subject of the work'.

This book all started because I was amazed at the lowliness to which soup had descended in the eyes (and stomachs) of most citizens. Soup was really only considered as winter fare, as a sort of healthy thing boiling merrily on the stove, that had to be eaten in the winter to keep away seasonal ills.

And restaurants often regarded soups as totally 'du jour'. Yesterday's leftovers thrown together without any imagination or a caterer's pack of instant soup brewed up with water, garnished with a sprig of parsley and given a French title to con the public.

No, soup is an all-year round food and good soup-making is just as much an art as good bread or cake-making, meat cookery or vegetable cookery. French gourmets in particular consider soup-making the ultimate accomplishment of the chef.

As a basic food, every country, every civilisation has had its famous soups. France has its pot-au-feu, America its black bean soup, Italy its minestrone, Russia its borsch, China its bird nest soup, New Zealand its toheroa soup, Britain its brown Windsor soup, Australia its kangaroo tail soup, Spain its gazpacho. Most of these classical soups have been included in this book.

Soups and stews are often inseparable. Many countries have what is known as soup-stews, which are all served primarily as soups, with the meat and vegetables sometimes being served on the side.

Soup has a very important reason to lead the meal. It stimulates the salivary glands and the gastric juices, by its moisture and, if it is a hot soup, by its heat.

Light soups are usually served at dinner before a variety of courses to put the diner in the right mood. Thicker soups are better served at lunch or by themselves as they are a 'theme' rather than an 'overture'.

The choice of soup is important. Since soup is often the overture it should set the scene for the meal, set the style of the meal and be in harmony with the rest of it. The French custom is to serve soup at dinner only. At lunch they would serve hors d'oeuvre. The two are not often both served at a meal but if they are the hors d'oeuvre is served before soup. The Chinese serve soup halfway and all through a meal. And fruit soups are served either before or after a meal.

The full spectrum of soups is staggering, from the usual meat and vegetable types to those based on such marvellous items as sunflower seeds, kiwifruit, cherries and brazil nuts. Soup can be a luxury dish like a Crayfish Bisque or a

Scallop Cream soup or it can be made on a very simple and economical basis from refrigerator scraps, leftovers and trimmings. And of course, with panache, this type of soup can also be in the gourmet class.

Remember the time when a good soup simmering on the stove and bread cooking in it filled the house with the comforting feeling of foods prepared lovingly and slowly instead of the instant no-fuss, no-mess, no-taste foods of today? And although soup must be one of the most versatile dishes, with the inroads of packet, instant, canned and dried soups, it surely must be one of the most abused. Ignore these flour and water concoctions and plan deliciously flavoured, beautifully seasoned and temptingly aromatic soups of your own.

Soups can be thick or thin, light or heavy, hot or cold, strong or weak, whatever you want them to be. The base ingredient of most soups is generally a stock, made either from beef, chicken, vegetables or fish. Refer to the first chapter, on Stocks. In some cases where the stock is not very important to the soup, instant stock can be used. To this stock is added whatever is to be used to give the soup its characteristic flavour. Extras can be added to improve the taste, the appearance and the colour, and suitable garnishes will often do all three of these things too (see the chapter on Soup Garnishes).

If you are opening a can of soup or doing something with a packet, please try and disguise that loathsome artificial flavour. Add some real vegetables or some finely chopped fresh herbs or dried herbs. The Herbs and Spices chapter will be of use here.

Soups are classified into two categories, clear soups and thick soups. The clear soups are *consommés* (jellied or liquid) and the thick soups come under a variety of headings. There are the smooth soups, the *cream*, *purée* and *veloute*, and the chunky soups, the *broths*, *chowders* and *bisques*.

A *cream* soup is smooth, with the addition of cream or a white sauce. A *purée* is a soup that has been puréed in the blender, mouli, food processor or sieve, and a *veloute* is prepared by first making a roux, then adding a white stock to make a white sauce base.

A *broth* is a meat and/or vegetable soup. It starts out life as having a thin base, *bouillon*, in which there are meat and vegetables. However, with long cooking time a broth will thicken itself considerably. A *chowder* is a thick soup usually of American origin and although it normally has a milk base containing seafood, there are also vegetable chowders. The name chowder comes from the French word *chaudiere* meaning a heavy soup pot. A *bisque* is always a thick soup of shellfish, or sometimes vegetables, although in earlier times it was made from poultry or game. The origin of the word is unknown. All thick soups are variations on these themes.

For this book the soups have mainly been categorised by the chief ingredient rather than the method of making them. The great attraction of soups is that they can usually be made well in advance of the meal and reheated, if served hot, just before serving. If served chilled, they remain in the refrigerator until being served.

The most pleasant way to serve soup for a formal meal is from a tureen, served at the table by a member of the household. Hot soup is best served piping hot in hot soup dishes and cold soup should be ice-cold in chilled dishes. Always serve the soup in bowls or containers that suit the style of the soup. A hearty meat and vegetable broth is great in large rough pottery bowls or a delicately smooth Crayfish Bisque is beautiful in fine china.

If wine is served with soup it should be at room temperature and of fairly high alcoholic content. Classic wines to server are either brown sherry or old madeira. The addition of wine to soup itself frequently enhances the flavour, but do not oversalt soups to which wine has been added as the wine intensifies the saltiness. Strongly flavoured meat soups are often improved by the addition of red wine. White wine adds zest to shellfish soups. And beer adds tang to bean, cabbage and vegetable soups. If adding fortified wine, sherry or port, it is best to put some in the soup bowl before pouring in the hot soup.

To remove fat from soup, if it is hot, use paper towels to soak up the surface fat. If you have time, cook and refrigerate the soup overnight, then remove the solidified fat. Remember though that a little fat adds a lot of flavour to the soup. And if using packet soup, always add a little butter or oil to give the soup background, as well as disguising it by the addition of fresh herbs or vegetables.

A blender is extremely useful in soup-making to make purées. A mouli will do the same thing but takes longer and a food processor tends to make a coarse purée. Not only are sieves laborious but only rarely are they necessary. Sieving is the only way to remove seeds from a soup. Tomato seeds if chopped in a blender make the soup pink rather than a glorious tomato colour — and if left in the soup become irritating.

There are many ways of thickening soup. If thickening is necessary to the soup, the method has been incorporated in the recipe. A word of warning though: never thicken a soup with flour just before serving. Flour takes at least 12 minutes to cook. And if in doubt about thickening soup, don't. The flavours are often much better if the soup does not contain a lot of starch, whether flour, cornflour, pea flour or arrowroot. Numbers of servings are given to suit each recipe but it is usual to allow 1 cup (250 ml) of soup per serving. Use judgement: if the soup is for a large banquet, then only a few mouthfuls would be served to each person, but for a substantial meal, much more than a cupful would be served.

Present the soup well. A suitable garnish can make a soup look so spectacular that it can even look too good to eat.

STOCKS

A rich soup, a small turbot; a saddle of venison; an apricot tart;
this is a dinner fit for a king.
Brillat-Savarin, *La Physiologie du Gout*

Good full-bodied stock is the foundation of many great soups. Stock can be specially made or it can be an amalgamation of juices made and saved from meat and vegetable cookery. Generally a stock is made by the simmering down of nutritious substances. And the odd thing about stock-making is that whereas almost every other kind of cooking calls for all things young and tender, stock uses aged vegetables and meats, which are more flavoursome. Because instead of making every effort to keep the juices inside the materials you are cooking, you want to extract and trap every vestige of flavour from them — in liquid form.

There are numerous ready-made stock preparations, the most popular being in the form of stock powder or stock cubes to be dissolved in water. Be wary of these as they are very salty and no seasonings should be added before tasting first. Where stock is an important part of the soup it is far better to use a good home-made stock. When you have the opportunity, make stock and freeze it for future use. Where recipes are given here suggesting a good stock, don't use instant stock as it will do nothing for the soup. Use a home-made one.

It is simple to turn an old chicken carcass into stock but a little more trouble to produce beef stock and a very smelly process to make fish stock. Vegetable stock need only be a collection of waters from cooking vegetables. Bones used in stock-making should always be chopped or cut, meat trimmed of excess fat, and vegetables after cleaning may be blended.

Good stock cannot be made quickly, so simmering is important. Alexander Dumas called this simmering *faire sourire le pot-au-feu*, to make the pot smile. There was a time, not so long ago, when a stockpot simmered on the kitchen stove of many households. Often these stockpots became culinary dustbins breeding bacteria. As a result stomachs suffered and the stockpot fell into disrepute.

Nowadays a large hotel or restaurant may keep a stockpot. It will be far more hygienic, and into it will go all the trimmings from meat, poultry and vegetables, leftovers and all the eggshells. If tended properly, an excellent consommé emerges at the turn of the tap.

Stock can be made and used the same day, but it is better if it is at least a day old.

Beef Stock

500 g shin beef, cut into small pieces
500 g marrow bones, cut up
2 carrots, quartered
2 onions, quartered
2 leeks, split
2 stalks celery, sliced
6 peppercorns
6 cloves
1½ tablespoons salt
bouquet garni (thyme, bay leaf and parsley)
2 litres water

Brown the meat and bones well in the oven. Temperature does not matter as long as the meat does not burn. Transfer the meat and bones and any juices to a saucepan and add the remaining ingredients. The water should barely cover the ingredients.

Bring to the boil, cover and simmer for about 4 hours. Should the liquid evaporate too much, add more water but do not weaken the stock. Allow to cool, then refrigerate overnight and remove the fat. A good stock should be jelly by now, so reheat it slightly to dissolve it, then strain the stock well, and remove any marrow remaining in the bones and add to the stock. The stock is now ready to use.

Vegetable Stock

500 g carrots
500 g onions
½ head celery
15 g butter
4 peppercorns
1 tablespoon tomato purée
2 litres water
salt

Quarter the carrots and onions and slice the celery. Brown them lightly in the butter in a large saucepan. Add the remaining ingredients. Bring to the boil, cover and simmer for about 2 hours. Strain the stock and it is ready to use. Remember that any leftover vegetable waters used in boiling or steaming vegetables can be used in stock too.

Chicken Stock

This should ideally be made from the giblets (neck, gizzard, heart and feet) if available. It is best to use the liver for a pate or something as it tends to impart a bitter flavour. Best of all is a packet of chicken necks or a pile of uncooked carcass offcuts.

What you will probably have, and what is very good and economical, is the leftover carcass of a cooked chicken; or you might just happen to have the leftover carcass of a boned chicken.

chicken carcass and/or giblets
1 onion, chopped
1 carrot, chopped
1 stalk celery, sliced
salt
peppercorns
cloves
bouquet garni

Put the chicken carcass or giblets in a saucepan, and half cover with water. Add the onion, carrot and celery. Add some salt and a few peppercorns, a few whole cloves and a bouquet garni, all fresh if you have them.

Cover and simmer very gently for 1 to 2 hours. If using a cooked carcass simmer for only 1 hour, otherwise the stock gets rather bitter. When cool enough, strain, rubbing as much of the vegetables through the sieve as possible and removing as much chicken from the bones as possible.

Chill in the refrigerator and remove the solidified fat before using.

Fish Stock

Fish heads, especially snapper heads, make a marvellous fish stock, but avoid heads and trimmings from strong-smelling fish. The backbone is good too and tails, skins and trimmings can also be used. Remove the gills from the heads as they tend to make the stock bitter. And note that the shells of crayfish, crab and prawns are all delicious additions.

The smell of the stock cooking is rather gruesome but the trouble is worth it all.

about 750 g washed fish heads, bones, tails, skins and trimmings
½ cup chopped onions
¼ cup chopped carrots
½ cup chopped celery
6 white peppercorns
4 cloves
bouquet garni
twist of lemon peel
½ cup dry white wine
water to cover

Place all the ingredients in a saucepan. Heat until the liquid begins to simmer and continue simmering, uncovered (no longer than 15 minutes, or a bitter flavour may develop). At the last minute add any oyster or shellfish juices, if on hand.

Strain and the stock is ready to use. It will keep for several days, covered, in the refrigerator, or for several weeks frozen.

LIGHT SOUPS

A light soup is better than a thick one, which clogs the appetite.
Habits of Good Society

Light soups are not reheated stocks, of dishwater consistency, but carefully made flavoursome soups designed to cleanse the palate and stimulate the appetite before a heavy main course or gargantuan feast. As mentioned before, these soups are the 'overture' to the meal, and none is intended as a complete meal on its own. Perhaps they could be a meal for invalids, or a snack.

Light soups can be thin or jellied and are usually based on a stock. This should be a good home-made one as its flavour will be predominant. But do not waste a beautifully prepared stock on the ignorant. If they are B-grade guests give them a soup using a stock out of a plastic container and keep the real stock for the discerning and appreciative.

Note that *bouillon* is a French term for stock or broth. When clarified it becomes *consommé*, a word for which there is no English translation. Consommé, the most ubiquitous of the light soups, is normally made from beef, but clarified chicken, fish and vegetable stocks can also be consommé. There are innumerable varieties both simple and elaborate, but all consommé must be limpid.

As opposed to all-in soups using deteriorated or scrap vegetables and other ingredients, light soups usually call for the best of ingredients, though they are not economically shattering, as the quantities are usually minimal. Make sure hot light soups are served in very well-heated bowls. Being mainly liquid they tend to lose their heat quickly. And like most soups they need a suitable garnish. Many chilled and fruit soups could be classed as light soups also.

Ale Soup

Surprisingly light and refreshing, this soup is delicious in mugs after a day at the beach. Alternatively, serve it before a large meat course or serve it after a large main course.

    750 ml ale
    juice of 1 small lemon
    several pieces of lemon peel
    1 stick cinnamon
    salt
    sugar
    1 tablespoon potato flour

In a saucepan combine the ale, lemon juice, lemon peel and cinnamon, and salt and sugar to taste. Heat until very hot, stirring continuously. When hot add 1 tablespoon potato flour or instant potato diluted with a little of the hot soup. Stir for about 1 minute. Serve with plain water crackers.

Serves 2–3.

Avgolemono

Greek egg and lemon soup is simple yet has a sophisticated flavour.

    6 cups well-seasoned chicken stock
    6 tablespoons cooked rice
    3 eggs
    juice of 1 large lemon
    salt and freshly ground black pepper
    thinly pared lemon rind

Heat the chicken stock to boiling, then remove from heat and add the cooked rice. Beat the eggs with the lemon juice, add about 1 cup of the hot stock to this mixture, little by little, stirring constantly, and when quite smooth pour this back into the soup and cook over the lowest possible heat for a few minutes, stirring briskly to incorporate the egg mixture thoroughly with the stock. When slightly thickened, correct the seasoning and serve garnished with thin strips of peeled lemon rind.

Serves 4–6.

Bacon and Egg Consommé

500 g bacon or ham bones
4 bay leaves
freshly ground black pepper
2 eggs
spring onions

Cover the bacon bones and bay leaves with water and simmer for about 1½ hours. Remove the bones and the bay leaves and return any pieces of meat clinging to the bones to the saucepan. Add water to make the stock up to previous level. Add a generous amount of freshly ground black pepper. Meanwhile, beat the eggs well and make into a large thin omelette in a frying pan with a little butter. Cool the omelette and cut into thin strips. Add to the soup and bring to the simmer. Serve garnished (most important for flavour) with finely chopped spring onion.
Serves 6–8.

Consommé Al Jerez

Sherry Consommé is so easy to prepare yet so elegant.

home-made chicken stock
salt and pepper
dry sherry to taste
garlic croutons

Heat the chicken stock and season to taste. Add dry sherry to taste and serve immediately, garnished with garlic croutons.

Basel Flour Soup

A traditional Swiss soup, served at the Basel Carnival, the first Monday after Ash Wednesday. It starts at 4 am to show off the elaborate illuminated costumes, and so to keep everyone warm in the cold of the morning this simple soup made from basic ingredients is served. And because everyone has been up all night preparing for the Carnival, it is also known as Hangover Soup.

    4 tablespoons butter
    8 tablespoons flour
    1½ litres water
    2 cubes beef stock
    salt
    1 bay leaf
    grated nutmeg
    grated cheese

Melt the butter in a saucepan. Add the flour and brown very carefully, stirring regularly, until coffee brown. Don't burn — it tastes horrible. Add 1½ litres water and remaining ingredients except the cheese. Simmer, covered, for 1 hour. Serve garnished with grated cheese to taste.
Serves 6.

Bean Curd Soup

Bean curd, tofu or bean cake is the name of a valuable complete protein product, of delicate cheese-like consistency and nutlike flavour. It is commonly used in both Japanese and Chinese cookery. It is made from soy beans and is usually used freshly made. This is a typical soup using bean curd.

    5 cups chicken stock
    1 small leek, finely sliced
    ½ tablespoon soy sauce
    50 g spinach, shredded
    1 teaspoon finely chopped root ginger
    1 fresh tofu, cut in small cubes
    salt

Bring the stock to the boil, add the leek, soy sauce and spinach and simmer for 5 minutes. Add the ginger and tofu and simmer for about a minute or until the bean curd comes to the surface. Add salt to taste. Serve in small bowls.
Serves 6–8.

Creamed Beer Soup

A sweetish and malty, interesting soup.

    2 cups light beer
    4 tablespoons sugar
    2 egg yolks
    1 tablespoon sour cream
    toast to serve

Bring the beer slowly to the boil with the sugar. In a bowl beat together the egg yolks and the sour cream until mixed thoroughly. Slowly beat in half the beer mixture then return to the saucepan. Carefully reheat to allow the liaison to thicken the soup. Do not allow to boil or egg and cream will curdle. Serve in pottery bowls or mugs with dry toast.

Serves 2.

Chinese Egg Soup

Start a Chinese meal the appropriate way.

    4 cups chicken stock
    2 eggs
    2 teaspoons soy sauce
    salt
    spring onions to garnish

Heat well-seasoned chicken stock (home-made?) to boiling. Dribble 2 eggs, well stirred, gradually into the stock, stirring constantly. Add 2 teaspoons soy sauce and salt to taste. Finely slice several spring onions and garnish the soup with these.

Serves 4–6.

Consommé

Consommé can be served as is, or in an infinite variety of combinations. Remember though that this soup is definitely not meant as a meal but as a prelude to a meal.

To clarify soup to make consommé put 6 cups home-made beef stock in a saucepan. The stock must be icy cold. Stir in 1 slightly beaten egg white and 1 crumpled egg shell. Bring the soup very, very slowly to a simmer without stirring. As the soup heats the egg brings to the surface a heavy crusty foam. Do not skim this but push it to one side of the saucepan so that you can check that the soup is simmering but not boiling. Simmer for 10–15 minutes. Move the saucepan carefully from the heat and let it stand for at least 10 minutes. Wring out a cloth in hot water and suspend it, like a jelly bag, over a large bowl. Again push the scum to one side and ladle the soup carefully, straining it through the cloth. Cool and refrigerate until ready to use.

Variations

To equal parts consommé and tomato juice add chopped parsley.
To equal parts consommé and chicken stock add dry sherry.
To equal parts consommé and cream cheese add curry powder.
To equal parts consommé and milk add whipped cream or minced fried onion and cream.
On consommé float a slice of lemon smothered with caviar.

Curry Soup with Rice

Winter or summer this soup is particularly good.

    2 teaspoons curry powder
    5 cups chicken stock
    75 g long grain rice, uncooked
    watercress to garnish

Mix the curry powder with a little of the stock to form a paste and gradually stir it into the remainder of the stock. Bring it to the boil then add the rice and simmer for 30 minutes. Garnish with watercress.
Serves 6.

Jellied Beetroot Consommé

1 cup beetroot juice
1 cup consommé or beef stock
1 tablespoon gelatine
salt and white pepper
1 cup finely chopped cooked beetroot
1 tablespoon lemon juice
sour cream to garnish

Combine and heat the beetroot juice and consommé. Sprinkle the gelatine over 2 tablespoons cold water then dissolve over boiling water. Add to the beetroot juice and consommé, allow to cool then season to taste and add the beetroot and lemon juice. Pour into a container and refrigerate until set.

Break the jelly up with a fork and serve in small bowls with a dollop of sour cream.

Serves 4.

Jellied Mushroom Soup

250 g mushrooms, sliced
¼ cup chopped celery
¼ cup chopped onion
1 tablespoon chopped green pepper
3 cups vegetable or chicken stock
1 tablespoon gelatine
salt and pepper
red and green pepper to garnish

In a saucepan place the mushrooms, celery, onion, green pepper and stock. Bring to the boil, cover and simmer until the vegetables are soft. Purée in a blender or food processor. Soften the gelatine in ¼ cup cold water and dissolve it over hot water. Stir into the mushroom purée and season well with salt and pepper. Chill and serve icy cold, chopped up, in small bowls. Garnish with thin strips of green and red pepper.

Serves 6.

Jellied Tomato Consommé

3 teaspoons gelatine
5 tablespoons hot water
600 ml tomato juice
1 teaspoon grated onion
1 strip lemon rind
2 tablespoons dry sherry
2 teaspoons Worcestershire sauce
salt and pepper
finely chopped parsley

Shower gelatine into hot water and stir until dissolved. Pour tomato juice into a saucepan and add the grated onion and the lemon rind. Bring just to the boil. Strain. Add dissolved gelatine, sherry and Worcestershire sauce. Leave until cold. Season with salt and pepper and then chill until softly set. Break up lightly with a fork. Spoon into 4 to 6 soup bowls and sprinkle each with chopped parsley.

Serves 4–6.

Jellied Wine Consommé

The flavour of this soup depends on the beef stock so make sure it is a good one, preferably home-made.

4 cups clear beef stock
1½ tablespoons gelatine
½ cup water
1 tablespoon sugar
1 cup dry red wine
salt and white pepper
lemon juice or tabasco sauce
chopped chives to garnish

Bring the beef stock to the boil and stir in the gelatine softened in the ½ cup water. Add the sugar and stir until dissolved. Remove from heat. Add the wine, salt and pepper to taste and lemon juice or tabasco sauce to taste. Chill until soup lightly sets. Whisk with a fork and serve in chilled bowls topped with chopped chives or spring onion tops.

Serves 6.

Long Soup

This classic Chinese soup is slightly thicker, and better, than most restaurants offer.

250 g lean pork
4 spring onions
¼ small cabbage
1 tablespoon oil
6 cups chicken stock
½ teaspoon grated root ginger
2 chicken stock cubes
1½ tablespoons soy sauce
salt and pepper
125 g fine egg noodles

Slice the pork into fine shreds, shred the cabbage finely and cut the spring onions into thin diagonal slices. Heat the oil in a wok or large frying pan, add the pork and cabbage and quickly fry for a few minutes, stirring constantly. Add the stock, ginger, stock cubes, soy sauce and salt and pepper to taste. Bring slowly to the boil, reduce the heat, add the spring onions and simmer for 10 minutes. Cook noodles in boiling salted water until tender, 5 or 6 minutes, then drain well.

To serve, place a spoonful of noodles in each bowl and ladle the hot soup over.
Serves 8.

Misoshiru

In Japan, bean paste is called *miso*. Miso is a paste made from fermented soy beans and is an important part of the Japanese diet. Variations of this soup are often included in the Japanese breakfast. The paste is highly nutritious and can be used as a flavouring for vegetable, fish and meat soups and stews. It is invaluable to a vegetarian diet.

3 cups good chicken stock
2½ tablespoons miso
1 fresh tofu (bean curd), cubed
2 spring onions, finely sliced
½ long white radish, sliced paper thin

Heat the stock to boiling. Crush the miso and add along with the other ingredients. Bring to the boil and serve when the bean curd comes to the surface.
Serves 4–6.

Mushroom and Bacon Consommé

An excellent aperitif before a large meat course.

    1 kg bacon bones
    6 bay leaves
    350 g medium mushrooms
    freshly ground black pepper

Cover well the bacon bones and bay leaves with water and simmer gently for about 1½ hours. Strain, return stock to saucepan, remove any meat from bones and add this to the stock. Bring stock up to the previous level with more water. Wash the mushrooms well and add these, whole, to the soup. Simmer for about 15 minutes or until mushrooms are tender. Add plenty of freshly ground black pepper. Allow about 2 mushrooms per person when serving. Serve with wafer thin brown bread.
    Serves 10-12.

Mustard Soup

A velvety smooth tangy soup. Use your favourite mustard whether it's mild or strong, smooth or coarse.

    2 tablespoons butter
    2 tablespoons flour
    3 cups chicken stock
    1 cup milk
    salt and white pepper
    1½ teaspoons onion juice
    2 egg yolks, beaten
    2 tablespoons prepared mustard
    3 tablespoons cream
    whipped cream to garnish
    finely chopped parsley to garnish

Melt the butter, stir in the flour and cook for a few minutes. Gradually add the chicken stock and milk and heat, stirring continuously until smooth and thickened. Season with salt and white pepper and the onion juice. In a bowl, combine the egg yolks, mustard and cream. Whisk in a cup of hot soup then return to rest of the soup. Reheat, but do not boil, and check seasonings.
    Garnish with dollops of whipped cream and finely chopped parsley. Note that this is also delicious chilled with half a cup of cream added.
    Serves 4.

Short Soup

Good chicken stock is essential for this classic Chinese soup.

Soup

8 cups chicken stock
3 spring onions, finely sliced
½ teaspoon sesame oil
1 chicken stock cube

Wontons

250 g pork mince
¼ small cabbage, finely shredded
1 tablespoon soy sauce
½ teaspoon sesame oil
1 teaspoon grated root ginger
25 wonton wrappers
1 egg, lightly beaten

To make the soup, in a saucepan combine the chicken stock, spring onions, sesame oil and the crumbled chicken stock cube, bring to the boil and simmer for three minutes.

To make the wontons, combine the pork mince, finely shredded cabbage, soy sauce, sesame oil and grated ginger and mix well. Place a teaspoon of the pork mixture slightly below centre of each wonton wrapper. Brush around edges of wrapper with lightly beaten egg. Fold the wrapper diagonally in half to form a triangle. Press edges to seal, pressing out any air pockets around the filling. Brush a dab of egg on the front right corner of each triangle and on the back of the left corner. With a twisting action bring the two moistened surfaces together. Pinch to seal. Drop the wontons into vigorously boiling salted water and cook for 15 minutes.

To serve, place 3 or 4 wontons in each soup bowl and pour the hot soup over. *Serves 6–8.*

Solyanka

Russian soups are often full of surprises and this one is a good example. It is light, astringent and an ideal start to a summer's meal.

1 large ham bone, chopped
6 peppercorns
3 whole cloves
a pinch mace
1 small onion, chopped
1 small carrot
1 stalk celery, sliced
bunch herbs such as thyme, marjoram and tarragon, or 1 teaspoon
   mixed herbs
sprig parsley
2 bay leaves
2 litres water

Combine the above in a large saucepan and simmer gently for 1½ hours. Allow to cool slightly then strain the consommé, pushing the vegetables through the strainer and putting in any pieces of ham. Return to saucepan and check for salt.

250 g preserved sauerkraut
1 tablespoon chopped parsley

Heat the ham consommé and just before serving add the sauerkraut and parsley. Heat through and serve immediately.
Serves 8–10.

Stout and Sour Cream Soup

Liquid velvet.

    500 g sour cream
    2 tablespoons flour
    1 teaspoon chopped spring onion
    1 teaspoon finely chopped parsley
    2 cups stout
    salt and white pepper

Smoothly blend the sour cream and flour in a saucepan. Add the spring onions and parsley. Gradually stir in the stout over low heat and cook until hot, without boiling, stirring all the time to prevent lumps forming. Season well with salt and white pepper.

Serve hot with rye or black bread.

Serves 4.

Stracciatella

Originally a Roman soup that is now common all over Italy. The success depends on the quality of the ingredients.

    4 cups chicken stock
    2 eggs
    2 tablespoons grated parmesan cheese
    1 tablespoon fine semolina

Put the chicken stock in a saucepan. In a basin, beat the eggs then mix in the parmesan cheese and semolina. Add one cup of the chicken stock to the egg mixture, mixing well. Heat the remaining stock and when it is almost boiling, pour in the egg mixture and beat it vigorously with a fork for 3 or 4 minutes, then leave the soup to barely come to the boil. The egg mixture should not be absolutely smooth, but just breaking up into tiny flakes. Serve quickly.

Serves 4.

Yoghurt Soup with Mint

An extremely refreshing sharp-sour taste. The barley can be omitted but it does give bulk to the soup.

¼ cup pearl barley
6 cups chicken stock
2 tablespoons grated onion
¼ cup finely chopped mint
3 cups plain yoghurt
salt
freshly ground black pepper

Place the barley in a small bowl, add water to cover and soak overnight. The next day drain the barley in a strainer and rinse well. Put in a saucepan with the chicken stock and grated onion. Bring to the boil, cover and simmer for 15 minutes or until barley is tender. While the barley is cooking, chop the mint, using only the tender leaves. (Dried mint will not do.)

When the barley is tender, remove from heat. Add the mint, then let cool to room temperature. Add the yoghurt and stir into the soup until smooth. Add salt and pepper to taste. Serve the soup icy cold.

Serves 8.

MEAT SOUPS

One wit, like a knuckle of ham in soup, gives a zest and flavour to the dish,
but more than one
Serves only to spoil the pottage.
Tobias Smollett, *The Expedition of Humphrey Clinker*

Meat soups are basically substantial soups — many being main course or lunch soups. Many meat soups are more a meat and vegetable affair with the meat providing the basis or the background to the soup. Here, the cheaper cuts of meat are usually the best, because they often have the best flavour and need long slow cooking — which most soups provide — to bring out the flavour. A ham bone, bacon bones, a piece of beef brisket or brisket bones, gravy beef, shin of beef, lamb shanks, lamb neck chops, scrag end of lamb or a piece of boiling bacon, all make good soups.

Offal soups are usually lighter and probably make more interesting soup for most as many people will not or cannot eat offal as it is but find it perfectly acceptable in soup form. Normandy Tripe soup, for instance, has fooled many a guest who would never have touched it if they had known it had been made from the most hateful of all offal, tripe. Although very few meat soups are all meat and nothing else, there are many examples where the meat is the predominant feature of the soup. Note that Mock Turtle soup is actually made from a calf's head.

Arabian Mutton Soup

A well-known Arabian soup known as Chervah, this is very rich and sufficing.

1 kg mutton neck chops
10 cups water
500 g tomatoes, peeled
750 g onions
chopped fresh mint
salt and ground black pepper
150 g vermicelli

In a large saucepan place the mutton neck chops with the water. Add the peeled tomatoes and the onions, previously peeled, sliced and slightly browned in oil and a good handful of chopped mint. Season highly with salt and ground black pepper, bring to the boil and simmer for 3 to 3½ hours. Allow to cool, then chill in refrigerator overnight. Remove the fat solidified on top and remove the meat from the chops (discarding bones and fat) and return the chopped meat to the soup. Reheat the soup and add the vermicelli broken into pieces and simmer until vermicelli is tender.

Serves 8.

Chilli con Carne

You have probably only had Chilli con Carne with rice as a main meal but in Texas where it originated it is often served as a soup in big bowls. Even then it is almost a meal in itself.

1 cup dried brown or red kidney beans
500 g minced beef
1 large onion, finely chopped
1 clove garlic, crushed
3 tablespoons oil
1 cup tomato sauce
¾ cup tomato purée
1½ teaspoons salt
½ teaspoon caraway seeds
1 bay leaf, crumbled
1 tablespoon medium chilli powder
1 tablespoon dried basil
beef stock
chopped onion to garnish
grated cheese to garnish

Soak the beans overnight. In the same water simmer gently, unsalted, for about an hour or until tender. In a large covered frying pan, gently fry the mince, onion and garlic in the oil until the mince is separated and browned. Add the tomato sauce, tomato purée, and seasonings and continue to simmer for about 10 minutes. Add the drained beans and simmer a further hour. As the mixture should be the consistency of thick soup, add beef stock or water as required. Serve in large bowls, garnished with finely chopped onion and grated tasty cheese and accompanied by chunks of brown bread.

Serves 4–6.

Chinese Pork and Vegetable Soup

peanut oil
1 cup lean pork
1 cup sliced mushrooms
½ cup diced carrot
1 cup sliced celery
6 cups chicken stock
½ cup shredded spinach
monosodium glutamate
1 egg
2 tablespoons cornflour
salt and pepper

In a little peanut oil gently fry the pork, cut into strips, until lightly browned. Add the sliced mushrooms, diced carrot and sliced celery. Continue to fry gently until vegetables are tender.

Add the chicken stock. Then add the finely shredded spinach and a pinch of monosodium glutamate. Bring to the boil, and add the egg, lightly beaten, stirring quickly. Add the cornflour made into a thin paste with a little cold water and simmer for a further few minutes. Season to taste with salt and pepper and serve hot.

Serves 6.

German Vegetable and Frankfurter Soup

A deliciously substantial winter soup.

5 cups chicken or beef stock
2 medium potatoes, peeled and diced
4 small leeks
250 g turnips
250 g carrots
1 stalk celery
125 g rindless bacon, chopped
6 frankfurters
salt and freshly ground black pepper
chopped parsley to garnish

Pour the stock into a large saucepan, add the diced potatoes, bring to the boil and simmer until tender. Purée the potato in the blender or food mill and return to the saucepan. Split the leeks in half lengthways and cut across in ½ cm slices. Wash them well. Peel and dice the turnips and carrots, slice the celery, and add the vegetables to the potato stock. Fry the chopped bacon until crisp and add the bacon and bacon fat to the saucepan. Bring the soup to a gentle simmer and cook for about an hour. Several minutes before serving, slice the frankfurters thinly and add to the soup. Season well and serve garnished with chopped parsley and accompanied by rye bread.

Serves 6–8.

Goulash Soup

500 g shin beef
2 tablespoons oil
1 large onion, chopped
2 tablespoons flour
1 tablespoon paprika
¼ teaspoon dried marjoram
½ teaspoon caraway seeds
1 clove garlic, crushed
420 g can peeled tomatoes or equivalent fresh tomatoes
4 cups beef stock
1 tablespoon tomato paste or concentrate
500 g potatoes, peeled and cubed
1 green pepper, seeded and chopped
salt and freshly ground black pepper

Trim and cut meat into very small pieces, then heat oil in a large saucepan and fry the meat over a high heat until well browned. Lower the heat, stir in the chopped onion and cook until lightly browned. Sprinkle in the flour, paprika, marjoram, caraway seeds and garlic. Stir well and cook for a minute or two before adding the tomatoes and stock. Bring to the boil, cover and simmer for about 45 minutes. Remove lid, add tomato paste, potatoes and chopped pepper and simmer, stirring occasionally, until meat and potatoes are tender.

Taste and correct seasoning and serve with a dollop of sour cream or yoghurt stirred into each bowl of soup. Dumplings go well, cooked on top of this soup.

Serves 4–6.

Corn and Frankfurter Chowder

Served in heated mugs with plenty of toast this is excellent fireside fare.

1 medium onion, chopped
1 tablespoon butter
2 tablespoons flour
salt and freshly ground black pepper
1½ cups chicken stock
450 g can cream-style sweet corn
¼ cup chopped parsley
4 frankfurters, finely sliced
2 cups milk
100 g grated tasty cheese

Gently fry the onion in the butter in a large saucepan. Stir in flour and seasonings. Add chicken stock, corn, parsley and frankfurters. Stir in milk. Heat to serving temperature but do not boil. Add the cheese and serve hot.
Serves 6–8.

Hare Soup

1 small hare, skinned, cleaned and jointed
200 g lean bacon
100 g butter
2 onions, peeled and chopped
12 peppercorns
1 blade mace
bouquet garni
3 litres stock or water
4 tablespoons flour
½ cup port wine
salt

Do not wash the hare but pat it dry with kitchen paper. Cut the bacon into small pieces. Heat half the butter in a large saucepan, add the hare pieces and bacon and fry on all sides until browned. Add the onions, peppercorns, mace, bouquet garni and water. Bring gently to the boil, lower the heat and simmer for 3 hours.

Strain the liquid and put the hare meat aside. Heat the remaining butter in another saucepan and add the flour, stirring the mixture until smooth and golden brown. Add the hare liquid, a little at a time, stirring constantly until it comes to the boil. When it boils add the port and salt to taste and cook gently for 20 minutes.

While it is cooking, cut off a little of the hare meat from the bones, shred and return it to the soup to reheat (the rest of the hare meat can be served another time as a main dish, reheated and served with mashed potatoes). Serve the soup hot with fingers of crisp toast.

Serves 10.

Kidney Soup

It might smell strange whilst cooking but this is quite a winner.

250 g kidney
5 cups beef stock
bouquet garni
25 g butter
1 onion, chopped
1 tablespoon flour
1 tablespoon tomato paste
salt and pepper
arrowroot
½ cup red wine
chopped parsley

Skin the kidney if necessary, core it and slice it up. Brown in its own juices, in a saucepan, stirring, then add half the beef stock and the bouquet garni. Cover and simmer until tender, about 1 hour. Remove bouquet garni and turn soup into a bowl.

In the same saucepan, melt the butter and fry the onion gently, until brown but not burnt. Stir in the flour and the tomato paste. Add the remaining stock, and kidney and kidney stock and simmer for 10 minutes. Season. Put the soup through a blender and return the purée to the rinsed-out saucepan. Reheat and thicken with a little arrowroot mixed with the red wine. Check seasoning. Serve garnished with chopped parsley.

Serves 4.

Lamb Curry Soup

250 g boneless shoulder of lamb, cut into small cubes
3 cups chicken stock
2 small onions, finely chopped
½ cup peeled, seeded and chopped tomato
4 teaspoons curry powder
1 tablespoon tomato paste
½ teaspoon salt
¼ teaspoon pepper
½ cup diced peeled apple
¼ cup diced banana
¼ cup raisins
¼ cup rice
2 tablespoons butter
¼ cup flour
1 cup cream
¾ cup milk

In a saucepan combine the lamb with 3 cups water, bring to the boil and simmer 5 minutes. Add the chicken stock, onion, tomato, curry powder, tomato paste, salt and pepper and simmer, covered, for 1½ hours. Add the apple, banana, raisins and uncooked rice. In a frying pan melt the butter and stir in the flour, and cook the roux over low heat, stirring, for a few minutes. Remove pan from heat and add 1 cup of the soup, whisking the mixture until smooth, and stir into the soup. Simmer for 15 minutes, or until the rice is cooked and stir in the cream and milk. Bring to the boil and add salt to taste.

Serves 4.

Liver and Bacon Soup

If you like liver, this soup is delicious. If you don't then forget it.

1 medium onion
100 g lean bacon
25 g butter
250 g ox or pig liver
2 tablespoons flour
4 cups water
½ teaspoon salt
1 tablespoon lemon juice
½ teaspoon Worcestershire sauce
chopped parsley

Finely chop the onion and bacon. Gently fry them in the butter in a saucepan for about 5 minutes. Cut the liver into small cubes; this is mostly easily done if you partially freeze the liver first. Toss the liver in the flour until each piece is coated. Add to the saucepan and fry with onion and bacon a further 5 minutes, stirring. Gradually blend in the water and add the salt, lemon juice and Worcestershire sauce. Bring slowly to the boil, stirring, then cover and simmer gently for 1½ hours. Purée in the blender, then return soup to rinsed saucepan. Reheat and check seasoning. Serve garnished with chopped parsley.

Serves 4.

Mexican Meatball Soup

A very popular soup in Mexico where it is known as Sopa de Albondigas.

    5 cups beef stock
    ¼ cup olive oil
    1 small onion, chopped
    1 clove garlic, crushed
    310 g can tomato purée
    350 g minced beef
    350 g minced pork
    ⅓ cup uncooked rice
    1 egg, beaten
    1½ teaspoons salt
    ½ teaspoon chilli powder
    ¼ cup chopped parsley

Use a good rich beef stock, preferably home-made. Heat the oil in a saucepan, and gently fry the onion and garlic until golden. Stir in the tomato purée and beef stock. Combine the minced beef, minced pork, rice, egg, salt and chilli powder. Shape into balls about the size of a walnut. When the stock is boiling briskly drop in the meatballs, cover, and cook over moderate heat for 30 minutes. Serve with chopped parsley strewn on top.

Serves 4–6.

Normandy Tripe Soup

This is a lovely soup that even tripe haters enjoy. Make sure the tripe is washday white when you buy it.

Cut washed tripe into very small pieces and pack them into a casserole with alternating layers of finely sliced carrots, finely sliced onions, and a good sprinkling of mixed herbs, some garlic and some salt and pepper. Make a good stock with beef cubes dissolved with dry cider and use this to cover the tripe.

Cook in low oven for several hours, not less than 2, and the longer the better. Serve with lots of fresh rye bread.

Oxtail Soup

A deliciously hearty soup that could be a meal in itself if served with chunky brown bread and a refreshing green salad.

1 oxtail, cut into pieces
3 tablespoons flour
2 tablespoons oil
2 litres beef stock
2 stalks celery
1 onion
2 carrots
1 turnip
bouquet garni
6 peppercorns
salt
2 tablespoons tomato paste
port
2 tablespoons lemon juice

Remove any excess fat from the oxtail pieces, dredge them in 1 tablespoon flour and brown well on all sides in the oil in a large saucepan. Add the beef stock and the vegetables, all chopped, the bouquet garni, peppercorns and some salt. Bring to the boil, cover tightly and simmer gently for 3–4 hours or until oxtail is tender, depending on the size of the tail. Cool, then chill in the refrigerator to solidify the fat. Remove the fat, reheat slightly to dissolve the jelly, then strain the stock. Remove the meat from the bones, cut it into neat pieces and add to the stock. Return to saucepan, add tomato paste and thicken with the remaining 2 tablespoons flour mixed with some port. Simmer gently for about 10 minutes. Check seasoning and just before serving stir in the lemon juice.

Serves 6–8.

Oxtail and Noodle Soup

1 kg oxtail
⅓ cup chopped spring onion
2 stalks celery
1 carrot
1 teaspoon salt
¼ teaspoon each of thyme, marjoram and pepper
⅛ teaspoon crushed rosemary
4 cups beef stock
⅓ cup dry red wine
1 tablespoon tomato concentrate
2½ cups egg noodles
salt and pepper

In a roasting dish roast the oxtail, cut into 5 cm pieces, in a pre-heated very hot oven (230°C) for 30 minutes. Add the chopped spring onion, including the green tops, the celery and carrot, both chopped, the salt, thyme, marjoram, pepper and crushed rosemary, stir the mixture and roast it for 10 minutes. Transfer the mixture to a large saucepan, add 2½ cups water to the roasting dish, and deglaze the dish over high heat, stirring and scraping up the brown bits clinging to the sides of the dish. Add the liquid to the saucepan with the beef stock and dry red wine combined with the tomato concentrate and bring the liquid to a boil over moderately high heat.

Reduce the heat to moderately low and simmer, covered, for 1½ hours. Simmer, uncovered, for 1½ hours more, or until meat is tender, and strain it through a colander into another saucepan. Discard the vegetables, remove the meat from the bones and chop it. Skim the fat from the broth, add the meat to the saucepan and bring the broth to a simmer. Add the egg noodles, boiled for 4 minutes, and simmer the soup for 3 minutes. Add salt and pepper to taste. Ladle into heated soup bowls.

Accompany with a crisp green salad.

Serves 4–6.

Philadelphia Pepper Pot

A famous American soup dating back to a harsh winter of 1777–78 when morale was low at Valley Forge. George Washington ordered his cook to make a good meal to cheer his troops but all the cook had were some tripe, some peppercorns and some seemingly useless scraps. However, an order was an order and the cook came up with this quite delicious soup, named after his home town. It does sound rather like Famine Food but it is really very good.

    1.5 kg tripe
    1 knuckle veal with meat left on
    1 kg marrow-bone, cracked
    2 large onions, sliced
    several sprigs parsley
    bay leaf
    2 sprigs thyme
    1 carrot, sliced
    ½ teaspoon crushed chilli pepper
    1 teaspoon whole allspice
    6 whole cloves
    4 potatoes, finely diced
    2 teaspoons dried marjoram
    2 tablespoons chopped parsley
    salt and freshly ground black pepper

Wash the tripe well, put in a saucepan with 2.5 litres water, bring to the boil and simmer for about 2 hours or until tender. Allow to cool in the broth. When cool enough to handle, cut into very small pieces and put broth in a container.

In the meantime, put the veal knuckle in another saucepan with 2.5 litres water. Remove the marrow from the marrow-bone with a knife or spoon and heat in a frying pan. Toss in the onions and gently fry until tender but not browned. Combine with the veal knuckle and the de-marrowed bone. Add the parsley, bay leaf, thyme, carrot, chilli pepper, allspice and cloves and cook over low heat, covered, until veal is tender, about 2 hours. Cool veal in broth until meat can be handled and chop veal in small pieces, discarding bones, and add to chopped tripe. Pour broth into a separate container and refrigerate both the meat and the two broths overnight. Next day, remove and discard fat from both broths. Combine the two broths and add the chopped tripe and veal, diced potatoes, marjoram and salt and plenty of pepper to taste. Cook over low heat for about 45 minutes. Add parsley. Note that if you are into dumplings, these can be cooked during the last stage.

Serves 12.

Poachers Broth

The Scots are certainly not a nation of poachers but this soup is very popular in Scotland. The combination of venison, hare and fresh vegetables is delicious.

Use leftover game or buy a small piece of venison, a piece of hare and a small piece of mutton. Cut the venison, mutton and hare (off the bone) into cubes and put in a saucepan with some barley and water to cover and a teaspoon or two of yeast extract. Simmer gently for an hour or so or until the meat is nearly tender. Add diced potatoes, diced turnip, diced carrots and some green beans and simmer until the vegetables are tender. Add some sliced mushrooms and enough tomato purée to give the soup a good colour. Simmer for a few minutes then season with salt and pepper and a little freshly grated nutmeg. Thicken, if you wish, with a little cornflour or potato flour mixed with a little water.

Pot-au-feu, Poule-au-pot or Petite Marmite

Pot-au-feu, *Poule-au-pot* or *Petite Marmite* are all more or less the same name for what is often called the national soup of France. Traditionally, Pot-au-feu was made with beef and chicken wings and giblets and Poule-au-pot with a chicken substituted for the wings and giblets. Petite Marmite is cooked in a *marmite*, an earthenware lidded pot higher than it is wide. All contain marrow-bone and seasonal, aromatic vegetables and all are usually served by starting with the clear soup and eating the meat and vegetables on the side or after the soup. The meat and vegetables can also be served in the soup. Hence it is often referred to as a knife-and-fork soup. The marrow-bone is tied in cheesecloth so it won't cloud the soup but will add good flavour. Blanched cabbage is often served as a side dish and toasted French bread is the accompaniment.

1 kg chuck steak, cut into chunks
1 medium chicken
1 marrow-bone (cut in two and tied in cheesecloth)
12 cups water
2 carrots
1 small turnip
3 leeks, white part only
3 stalks celery
1 whole onion stuck with 10 cloves
bouquet garni
salt
toasted French bread

In a large saucepan place the beef, chicken, marrow-bone and water. Bring slowly to the boil and skim off foam. Peel the carrots and turnip and cut them into chunks. Cut the leeks and celery into chunks and add to the saucepan. Add the onion stuck with cloves and a bouquet garni comprised of 2 sprigs parsley, 2 sprigs thyme, a bay leaf and the leaves of a stalk of celery, tied together with cotton. Add some salt. Bring back to the boil, skim again, cover and cook slowly 2½ to 3 hours on the stove or in the oven. The soup should be clear. Remove the bouquet garni. Add salt to taste (it might need a lot), and serve as described previously. Either start with the clear soup and serve the meat, chicken, vegetables and marrow from the bone separately, or serve all together in bowls. Accompany with toasted French bread.
Serves 8–10.

Scotch Broth

There are many versions of this traditional Scottish soup. Here is a good, basic one.

    700 g neck of mutton
    9 cups water
    salt and pepper
    1 carrot, peeled and chopped
    1 turnip, peeled and chopped
    1 onion, peeled and chopped
    2 leeks, thinly sliced
    3 tablespoons pearl barley
    finely chopped parsley

Cut up the meat and remove any fat. Put it in a saucepan with the water and add salt and pepper. Slowly bring to the boil. Cover and simmer 1½ hours. Add the neatly chopped vegetables and the barley. Cover and simmer for about 1 hour until the vegetables and barley are soft. Remove any fat from the surface with a spoon or with kitchen paper or better still, refrigerate overnight and remove fat before reheating. Serve the soup garnished with parsley.

Turkish Tripe Soup

500 g tripe
5 cups water
100 g butter
salt and pepper to taste
4 cloves garlic
⅓ cup white wine vinegar
1 egg
1 teaspoon mild chilli powder

Wash tripe well, cut into 0.5 cm pieces and place in a saucepan with the water, butter, salt and pepper. Cook until tender. If it is thought there is not enough broth you may add another cup of water. When cooked, remove from heat.

In a cup, crush the four cloves garlic or put them through a garlic press into a cup, add the vinegar and slowly beat in the egg. Stir this mixture gently into the tripe soup. Check seasoning and pour soup into a tureen.

In a saucepan melt 1 tablespoon butter and add the chilli powder and mix well. Mild paprika may be used if the thought of chilli powder is too strong. Pour this mixture gently over the soup and serve. If desired, chopped parsley may be added over the red butter and chilli mixture. This is a delicious winter soup. Serve it with a hot French loaf.

Serves 6.

Turkish Wedding Soup

A delicious lamb soup that is unusually refreshing.

1 kg lamb shanks (knuckles)
seasoned flour
1 tablespoon oil
3 tablespoons butter
6 cups water
1 onion, quartered
1 carrot, grated
salt and pepper
3 egg yolks
¼ cup lemon juice
1½ teaspoons sweet paprika
cayenne pepper

Have your butcher crack the lamb shanks. Dredge the shanks in seasoned flour and in a saucepan brown them in 1 tablespoon each of oil and butter. Add the water, bring to the boil, and skim off the froth. Add the onion and carrot, and some salt and pepper. Simmer the mixture, covered, for 2 hours or until the lamb is tender. Let the mixture cool and chill overnight.

Skim the fat, heat the mixture and strain it through a sieve into a saucepan. Push as much of the vegetables through the sieve as possible, discard the rest. Remove the meat from the bones, chop it into small dice and add to the saucepan. In a bowl beat the egg yolks with the lemon juice, stir in 1 cup of the hot broth, then stir the mixture into the broth. Heat the soup but do not boil. In a small frying pan melt the remaining 2 tablespoons butter, remove the pan from the heat and stir in the paprika and a dash of cayenne pepper. Ladle the soup into heated bowls and garnish each serving with a swirl of the paprika mixture.

Serves 4–6.

Cream of Veal Soup

8 tablespoons butter
⅓ cup flour
5 cups chicken stock
250 g lean veal, cubed
2 egg yolks
½ cup cream
½ cup cooked macaroni
1 tablespoon parsley
parmesan cheese

In a saucepan melt 6 tablespoons of butter and stir in the flour. Cook the roux over a low heat, stirring, for a few minutes. Remove pan from heat and add the chicken stock, heated, in a stream, stirring. Simmer over moderate heat, stirring occasionally, for 10 minutes.

In a frying pan, gently fry the veal in 2 tablespoons butter for 5 minutes, then add to the saucepan along with the pan juices. Simmer, over low heat, stirring occasionally, for 1½ hours.

Transfer the veal mixture to a blender, in two batches, purée it and return to the cleaned saucepan along with enough water to make soup up to original amount before evaporation. Bring the soup just below the simmer.

In a bowl combine the egg yolks with the cream and add it to the soup, whisking, for 5 minutes, or until it is thickened. Remove saucepan from heat and add macaroni, chopped into small pieces, and parsley. Serve, if desired, with grated parmesan cheese.

Serves 4.

Venison Soup

500 g stewing venison with bones
1 rasher bacon
1 stick celery, cut in three
1 medium onion, quartered
1 medium carrot
bouquet garni (3 sprigs parsley, 1 bay leaf, 2 sprigs thyme)
¾ teaspoon mace
6 cups water
1 tablespoon butter
1 tablespoon flour
½ cup port
salt and pepper

Put everything except the butter, flour and port into a large saucepan. Simmer for about 2 hours until the venison is cooked. The time depends on the age of the venison. Skim and strain the soup. Pick a few nice pieces of meat out of the strainer and keep them warm. Put the rest of the meat, without skin and bones etc. back in the soup and purée in a blender or food processor. Bring back to the boil, turn down the heat and add the butter and flour, that have been worked together, in small knobs. Keep stirring as you do this and the soup will thicken smoothly after a few minutes. Do not boil the soup, barely simmer it. Add the port and the pieces of venison and season with salt and pepper. Serve very hot in hot bowls. Garnish with parsley if you wish.

Serves 6.

POULTRY SOUPS

Worries go down better with soup than without.
Yiddish Proverb

Probably the most popular of all soups is a good chicken soup. A leftover chicken carcass from a roast dinner perhaps, can be very easily made into a stock or soup with the addition of vegetables, herbs and spices. Never cook a pre-cooked carcass for more than an hour otherwise it tends to become bitter. Giblets and necks are ideal for chicken stock too. And save unwanted backs, giblets and necks. Keep adding to them in the freezer until you have enough to make a delicious chicken soup.

Chicken lends itself to many combinations, some of them classics. It tastes good with sweet corn, noodles, celery, herbs, curry and coconut for instance.

Pheasant, duck, turkey, guinea fowl or the gamier swan, goose, pigeon or pukeko can be substituted in most chicken soup recipes. Beware of using the very dark meat as this can be too strong even for the bravest stomach.

Remember too that if you strip and dice the meat from a cooked chicken don't then cook it for too long otherwise the flesh will disintegrate into unappealing strings. Chicken Noodles soup is simply well-seasoned chicken stock with plenty of short thin noodles added, a soup that is a favourite of all packet-soup bashers.

Golden Chicken soup is a favourite Jewish soup served on the Sabbath Eve on all Jewish tables. It has a variety of garnishes and is made from a whole chicken, simmered with a variety of root vegetables. The name comes from the rounds of golden fat which float on the surface after the soup has been strained.

Chicken and Avocado Soup

This soup is to Mexico City what Onion soup is to Paris. Sometimes this delicate soup is served with rice and slices of hot pepper along with the avocado.

    6 cups chicken stock
    1 whole chicken breast
    2 onions, finely sliced
    ½ teaspoon ground coriander
    ½ teaspoon oregano
    ½ teaspoon salt and pepper
    freshly ground black pepper
    1 very ripe avocado

In a large saucepan combine the chicken stock, chicken breast, onions and seasonings. Bring to the boil, cover and simmer until the chicken is tender. Remove the chicken from the stock and discard the onions from the stock. When the chicken is cool enough to handle remove the skin and bones and cut the meat into thin julienne strips. Just before serving stir the chicken into the stock and heat. Check the seasoning. Peel the avocado, cut it into thin slices and add to the soup. The slices will float on top.
    Serves 6.

Chinese Chicken and Bean Sprout Soup

Don't overcook.

    1 tablespoon oil
    1 onion, peeled and chopped
    2 tablespoons flour
    5 cups chicken stock
    200 g chicken, cooked and finely diced
    1 tablespoon soy sauce
    2 carrots, scraped and cut into matchsticks
    250 g bean sprouts
    ¾ cup finely diced cucumber
    100 g mushrooms, finely sliced

Lightly fry the onion in the oil in a saucepan for 5 minutes. Stir in the flour and stock. Bring to the boil and add the chicken, soy sauce and carrots. Simmer 10 minutes. Add the bean sprouts, cucumber and mushrooms 3 minutes before serving. Check seasoning.
    Serves 6–8.

Cream of Chicken Soup

So smooth and creamy and full of chicken.

1 kg chicken pieces
6 cups water
2 stalks celery, sliced
1 bay leaf
1 small onion studded with 3 cloves
1 teaspoon salt and pepper
10 black peppercorns
1 cup cream
1 cup milk
50 g butter
4 tablespoons flour

Place the chicken pieces in a large saucepan, cover them with 6 cups water. Add the celery, bay leaf, onion, salt and peppercorns, bring to the boil, cover and simmer the chicken until the meat is falling off the bones. Strain the stock and detach the meat from the bones, discarding the skin, bones, vegetables and flavourings. Return the strained stock to the saucepan and add the cream and milk. Bring the soup to simmering point. Work the flour into the softened butter to make a *beurre manie*, break into small pieces and drop one by one into the simmering soup, stirring constantly. When the soup is smooth and thickened, add the chicken meat and heat through. Serve garnished with chopped chives and paprika.
Serves 6.

Chicken Liver Soup

Superbly rich and very tasty.

2 tablespoons butter
4 tablespoons flour
5 cups chicken stock
250 g chicken livers
marjoram
salt and white pepper
½ cup sweet sherry
chopped parsley

Make a roux with the butter and flour. Slowly add the chicken stock and cook until smooth and thickened. Rub the chicken livers through a sieve and add to soup. Cover and simmer for 15 minutes. Strain. Add a little marjoram and check seasoning. Add sherry, bring back to boil and serve very hot, garnished with parsley.

Serves 6.

Chicken Gumbo

Gumbo is an African name for okra and it also means a Creole thick soup-stew containing okra.

1 chicken
¼ cup bacon drippings
4 cups boiling water
2 cups peeled and seeded tomatoes
½ cup whole kernel corn
1 cup sliced okra
1 large green pepper, seeded and finely chopped
¼ cup finely chopped onion
¼ cup rice
½ teaspoon salt
2 tablespoons quick-cooking tapioca
5 cups water

Cut the chicken into pieces and dredge it with flour. In a saucepan brown it in the bacon fat then pour over the boiling water and simmer, uncovered, until the meat falls off the bones. Strain the stock and reserve and chop the meat. In a large saucepan place the vegetables, rice, salt, tapioca and 5 cups water and simmer, uncovered, for about 30 minutes or until the vegetables are just tender. Add the stock and chicken meat and check the seasoning. Heat to serve.
Serves 10–12.

Curried Chicken and Cauliflower Soup

6 cups chicken stock
2 onions, chopped
1 medium cauliflower, cut into pieces
1 cup chopped celery leaves
1 carrot, chopped
1 tablespoon curry powder
salt to taste

To the chicken stock in a saucepan add the vegetables and curry powder and simmer gently, covered, until the vegetables are tender. Purée in a blender, mouli or sieve. Add salt to taste and reheat before serving.
Serves 8.

Chicken and Olive Soup

25 g butter
½ teaspoon paprika
¼ cup flour
4 cups chicken stock
125 g black olives, pitted and chopped
1 cup (tightly packed) shredded cooked chicken
salt and pepper
lemon slices to garnish

Melt the butter in a saucepan, add the paprika and flour and stir until smooth. Gradually add the stock and bring to the boil, stirring. Simmer for 5 minutes. Add the olives and chicken. Bring to the simmer again and season to taste with salt and pepper. Serve with a slice of lemon in each bowl and accompanied by rye bread.
Serves 4–6.

Cock-A-Leekie

One of the most famous of Scottish dishes, it is called Cock-a-leekie because normally an old cock rooster is used. The idea of using prunes is very old and very good.

1 boiling fowl
a large veal or beef marrow-bone
a mixed bunch of parsley, thyme and bay leaf
3 rashers bacon, chopped
12 leeks
water to cover
salt and pepper
1 cup pitted prunes

Put the whole chicken, the chopped bones, herbs, bacon and all the leeks (except two) chopped into a large saucepan with water to cover well. Simmer, covered, until chicken is tender, a few hours. Top with water but don't weaken stock too much. Season to taste, strain, cut the chicken meat from the bones, spoon out the marrow-bones, and add to the soup. Allow to cool, refrigerate and remove fat. When ready to serve, add the remaining chopped leeks and the prunes, then simmer gently for no more than 15 minutes. A meal in itself with a healthy coarse bread.

Mulligatawny Soup

Very smooth, subtly flavoured and extremely filling.

1 small chicken
1 onion, sliced
50 g butter
2 teaspoons curry powder
½ cup flour
7 cups chicken stock
1 small apple
2 cloves
salt and pepper
juice of 1 lemon
3 tablespoons cream
1 cup cooked rice

Joint chicken and gently fry in a saucepan with the onion in the butter. Stir in the curry powder and the flour. Gradually add the stock to the contents of the saucepan, stirring well. Add the peeled and chopped apple, cloves and salt and pepper and simmer gently for an hour. Remove the cloves.

Lift the chicken from the soup. Remove all bones and dice flesh. Return pieces of chicken to soup and add lemon juice, cream and rice. Heat through and serve. The rice can be served separately if desired.

Serves 6.

Duck Soup

This soup can be made from any game bird — pheasant, goose, turkey, swan or whatever.

Using the carcass of the duck together with any gravy or juices left over from cooking the bird, or any unwanted part of the bird that would be suitable for making stock, necks, backs, etc., make a rich stock as per Chicken Stock (see page 17).

Strain and cool and remove any fat that solidifies. Finely chop an onion and a small turnip and finely slice a carrot, a leek and a stalk of celery. In a saucepan gently stew the vegetables in 3 tablespoons butter for 10 minutes without browning. Add the duck stock and simmer gently, covered, for about 45 minutes. Season with salt and pepper and serve piping hot with toast croutons.

A whole bird can also be used to make this soup. Make the stock with the jointed bird. Strain and, when cool enough, remove and cut all the white meat from the bones and return the meat to the stock, then proceed as before.

The Sultan's Chicken Soup

This is a very creamy coconut and chicken soup with a light spicy flavour. It makes a superb summer meal followed, perhaps, by fresh fruit salad.

1 medium chicken
10 cups water
50 g butter
5 large onions
4 cloves garlic
5 cm piece root ginger
2 teaspoons turmeric
¼ teaspoon chilli powder
4 heaped tablespoons pea flour
1 cup coconut cream
chopped parsley
450 g egg noodles
1 packet crisp fried noodles
4 hard-boiled eggs
1 bunch spring onions
chilli sauce
lemon wedges

Place the chicken in a large saucepan, add the water and cook the chicken, covered, until tender. When cooked, allow to cool in the water, remove the chicken and cut the meat from the bones. Reserve the chicken stock.

Chop the onions and crush or finely chop the garlic and ginger. In a large saucepan, heat the butter and fry the onions, garlic and ginger. When they begin to brown, add the turmeric and the chilli powder, then pour in the chicken stock (4 chicken stock cubes can be added for extra flavour). Cover and simmer 30 minutes.

Meanwhile, put the pea flour (available from health food shops) in a bowl and add a little cold milk, mixing until you have a smooth paste. Add more milk to make it fairly liquid, then stir it into the stock. Bring back to the boil and turn heat down to simmer.

Add the chicken meat to the soup and also the coconut cream. Add salt to taste and just before serving add a good handful of chopped parsley.

Accompaniments
1. Cook the egg noodles according to the directions on the packet.
2. Hard boil the eggs, then chop them.
3. Slice the spring onions, using the green part too.

To serve the soup, spoon about 1 large spoonful of egg noodles into each bowl and ladle the hot soup over. The accompaniments are the chopped eggs, the sliced spring onions, the crisp fried noodles and the chilli sauce, which should all be served in bowls. All guests to help themselves to the accompaniments, sprinkling these over the top. Pass around the lemon wedges for people to squeeze into the soup.
Serves 8–10.

Pennsylvanian Chicken Corn Soup

1 medium chicken
1 onion, chopped
5 cups water
salt and freshly ground black pepper
450 g can cream-style sweet corn
½ cup chopped celery with leaves
2 hard-boiled eggs, chopped

Rivels

1 cup flour
pinch of salt
1 egg
milk

Joint chicken and place in saucepan with the onion, water and some salt and pepper. Bring to the boil, reduce the heat and simmer, covered until chicken is tender. Remove chicken from stock and when cool enough to handle, strip meat from the bones. Discard bones and skin and cut into bite-sized pieces. Return chicken to the stock and refrigerate if you wish, to set the fat in order to remove it easily. Reheat soup, add the corn and celery. Continue simmering for 30 minutes and prepare rivels.

To make the rivels, combine the flour, salt, egg and enough milk to make a crumbly mixture. Mix with a fork or your hands until the crumbs are the size of small peas. Drop rivels and chopped eggs into soup. Cook 15 minutes, then adjust seasoning.
Serves 6.

VEGETABLE SOUPS

Only the pure in heart can make good soup.
Beethoven, 1824

Needless to say, there are more vegetable soups than any other category simply because there are more types of vegetables than any other form of food. There are at least forty different soup vegetables, which give just as many soups, plus all the various combinations with other vegetables and other foods. The combinations themselves are almost endless.

Very few soups could be made without the use of vegetables. For instance, most soups contain at least a member of the onion family for flavouring. And here again, the swing towards healthy foods has also made vegetable soups more popular than ever. And vegetable soups have vegetables that could never grace the dinner table as fresh vegetables but as soups can be made into gourmet delights. It is interesting too that a vegetables, used in a soup, can taste quite different depending on whether it is in big chunks, finely chopped or puréed.

Vegetarians can easily use this chapter by substituting vegetable stock for chicken or meat stock wherever necessary.

Avocado Soup

A most ambrosial soup. The mace sprinkled on top helps to minimise the richness without spoiling the smoothness.

    2 large, ripe avocados
    4 cups chicken stock
    300 ml cream
    salt and white pepper
    extra whipped cream
    ground mace

Peel and stone the avocados, mash them and put them into the chicken stock. Heat, then stir in the cream. Put the mixture through a sieve to remove any lumps, then return it to the saucepan, adding salt and white pepper to taste. Bring slowly to simmering, but do not boil. Serve immediately with a spoon of whipped cream and a sprinkling of mace in each bowl.

Serves 6.

Benevolent Soup

Sounds like something you'd get in a poorhouse — but it's extremely delicious, easy to make and uses winter root vegetables.

Ideally, peel and dice fairly finely, a couple of carrots, a couple of onions, a few Brussels sprouts or some cabbage, a couple of white turnips and a little swede turnip. Otherwise use up all the vegetables in the vegetable rack. Sweat them in some butter until the onions go transparent, then cover well with any good stock and simmer gently until the vegetables are tender. Season with salt and pepper and eat.

Korean Bean Sprout Soup

500 g bean sprouts
250 g lean beef cut into thin strips
2 teaspoons roasted sesame seeds
1 tablespoon sesame oil
3 cloves garlic, finely chopped
pepper
7½ cups water
2 spring onions, chopped, using the green part too
3 tablespoons soy sauce

Wash and drain the bean sprouts. Mix the meat with the sesame seeds, oil, garlic and pepper in a saucepan and cook over a moderate heat until the meat changes colour. Add the water, bring this to the boil and cover and simmer for 30 minutes. Add the spring onions and bean sprouts, cover and continue cooking for a few minutes. Just before serving, add the soy sauce and cook for another 5 minutes.
    Serves 6.

Borsch

There are almost as many spellings for this aristocrat among soups as there are recipes. It is the national soup of both Russia and Poland, is internationally famed, and varies as much as a recipe can. There are thick and thin borschs as well as hot and cold. Generally borsch contains beetroot and all borschs are served with a sour cream garnish.

This recipe is very substantial and ideal on a cold winter's night accompanied by black bread and red or white wine.

2 kg fresh beef brisket, cut into chunks
½ small cabbage, chopped
1 onion, chopped
3 carrots, cut into matchsticks
1 parsnip, cut into matchsticks
3 cooked beetroot, cut into matchsticks
the water in which the beetroot were cooked
salt and freshly ground black pepper
2 bay leaves
1 clove garlic, crushed
1 cup tomato purée
3 potatoes, cubed

Put the meat with bones in a large saucepan, cover with water and boil 1 hour. Allow to cool. Strain the liquid through a sieve, remove the skin and bone from the meat and cut into pieces. Ideally the liquid should be refrigerated to remove the fat. Return meat and liquid to the saucepan and add the prepared cabbage, onion, carrots, parsnip and beetroot, the beetroot water, salt and pepper, bay leaves and garlic. Simmer for 1 hour. Add the tomato purée and potatoes, adjust the seasoning and simmer another ½ hour. Garnish each bowl with a teaspoon of sour cream.

Serves 12.

Red Borsch

1 large raw beetroot
1 carrot
1 onion
1 clove garlic
2 stalks celery
5 cups beef stock
2 teaspoons vinegar
salt and pepper
sour cream

Grate the peeled beetroot, carrot and onion. Crush the garlic and finely chop the celery. Add the stock and simmer for about an hour. Season to taste and add the vinegar. Serve either very hot or chilled, and add a large blob of sour cream to each dish when serving. Extra vinegar may be added to suit personal taste.

Serves 4–6.

Brown Windsor Soup

Not so long ago a popular soup (well, it appeared on nearly every menu in England so someone must have eaten it!) was Brown Windsor. It was thick and brown and tasted vaguely like roast dinner.

It is made from thick gravy and leftover vegetables and cooked a long, long time until the vegetables disintegrate and the whole thing becomes thick and brown. It is then seasoned and diluted with stock or water if too thick. It can be puréed to hasten the mushing process but if left to cook for a while, will do this itself. Don't add herbs or other flavourings as that will spoil the simplicity of this very English soup. It is an excellent way to deal with leftovers, but don't serve it too often!

Broad Bean Soup

An excellent way to use older, large broad beans — or young ones of course.

25 g butter
1 medium onion, chopped
2 tablespoons flour
4 cups chicken stock
500 g shelled broad beans
salt and white pepper
grated rind and juice of 1 small lemon
4 tablespoons finely chopped parsley
whipped cream

Melt the butter in a large saucepan, add onion and cook slowly until soft. Stir in the flour and gradually stir in the stock. Chop the broad beans coarsely and add to the saucepan with seasoning, lemon rind and juice, and half the parsley. Bring to the boil, cover and simmer until beans are tender, about 40 minutes. Purée in blender. Return the purée to saucepan and reheat. Swirl in the cream and garnish with the remaining parsley before or after serving.

Serves 4–6.

Brussels Sprouts Soup

We all know about leftovers making good soups and here's a soup using cooked Brussels sprouts that no one would guess were from the night before.

½ chopped onion
25 g butter
2½ cups milk
2 cups chopped cooked Brussels sprouts
1½ cups chopped cooked potatoes
salt and freshly ground black pepper
freshly grated nutmeg

Soften the onion in the butter for 10 minutes, taking care not to brown it. Warm the milk and mix with the cold vegetables and the cooked onion. Blend to a purée in the blender. Season with salt and pepper and freshly grated nutmeg, and reheat to serve.

Serves 6.

Cabbage Soup

Surprise, surprise, the addition of sour cream to this cabbage soup makes it quite palatable indeed.

    1 small cabbage
    1 medium onion
    25 g butter
    2½ cups beef stock
    salt and white pepper
    sour cream
    chopped parsley

Shred the cabbage finely, wash well and drain. Coarsely grate the onion, and fry it in the butter in a saucepan until soft but not browned. Add the cabbage and stock and bring to the boil. If too thick add more stock. Season with salt and pepper, cover and simmer gently for 15 minutes. When serving stir a tablespoon of sour cream into each bowl and sprinkle with parsley.

Serves 4.

Callaloo

Callaloo is a type of spinach popular in the West Indies. It is also the name given to a soup-stew. If you do not wish to purée this soup, slice all the ingredients very finely and serve like that.

    1 kg spinach, silver beet or taro leaves, coarsely chopped
    4 cups water
    250 g okra, sliced
    250 g ham or a ham bone
    4 spring onions, chopped
    1 green chilli pepper, seeded and chopped
    1 clove garlic, crushed
    2 tablespoons chopped parsley
    ½ teaspoon thyme
    salt and pepper

Combine all the ingredients in a saucepan, bring to the boil, cover and simmer for about 1 hour. If a ham bone is used, discard it. Remove and chop the ham and return it to the soup. Purée the soup in a blender and return to the saucepan. Reheat before serving. If the soup is too thick, thin with some chicken stock.

Serves 6.

Cream of Carrot Soup

Serve this simple soup with lots of garlic bread.

500 g fresh young carrots
3 sprigs thyme
1 medium onion, finely chopped
75 g butter
4 cups chicken stock
4 tablespoons raw rice
1 cup milk
salt and white pepper
parsley to garnish

Scrape and slice the carrots and place in a saucepan with the thyme, onion and 50 g butter. Cook, covered, very slowly for 20 minutes, shaking the saucepan occasionally. Add the chicken stock and rice and simmer gently until the rice is cooked and the carrots are soft.

Put through a blender, mill or sieve. Return the purée to the saucepan, add 1 cup milk — or milk and cream — 25 g butter, salt and plenty of white pepper to taste. Reheat and serve garnished with chopped parsley.

Serves 6.

Carrot and Lemon Soup

Lemon gives the carrot an unexpected tang.

2 tablespoons oil
1 medium onion, finely chopped
1 kg carrots, scraped and chopped
6 cups chicken stock
grated rind and juice of 1 lemon
salt and white pepper
chopped parsley

Heat the oil in a large saucepan and gently fry the onions and carrots, stirring occasionally, for 5 minutes. Stir in the stock, lemon juice, half the lemon rind and bring to the boil. Simmer for 40 minutes until the carrots are very tender. Purée the mixture in a blender. Return the purée to the saucepan, add the remaining lemon rind and season with salt and white pepper. Reheat the soup and cook, stirring, for 5 minutes. Check seasoning. Sprinkle with parsley and serve with plain crackers.

Serves 6.

Mexican Carrot Soup

The tang of garlic gives carrot a marvellously elegant lift.

    500 g young carrots
    5 cups chicken stock
    3 cloves garlic, crushed
    salt and black pepper
    1 cup milk or ½ cup cream
    chopped parsley

Scrub and slice the carrots and cook them until tender in the chicken stock. Blend in a blender. Return the purée to the saucepan and add the garlic, and salt and freshly ground black pepper to taste. Add the milk or cream. Heat to blend but do not boil. Just before serving stir in a good handful of finely chopped parsley.

If serving hot, garnish with some garlic croutons. If serving cold, chill well and swirl a dollop of whipped cream into each bowl.

Serves 6–8.

Cream of Cauliflower Soup

    1 medium cauliflower
    50 g butter
    4 tablespoons flour
    4 cups chicken stock
    1 onion, finely chopped
    1 stalk celery, finely sliced
    2 sprigs parsley, chopped
    ½ cup cream
    nutmeg ¼ tsp
    salt and white pepper ¼ tsp
    chopped parsley and chopped raw cauliflower to garnish

Cut the cauliflower into large flowerets, peel the stalk and chop. Reserve a little cauliflower for garnish. Melt the butter in a saucepan and stir in the flour and cook, stirring to form a smooth paste. Gradually add the chicken stock, then the onion, celery and parsley. Simmer for 20 minutes. Strain the stock, add the cauliflower and cook until cauliflower is soft. In a blender, purée the soup then return it to the cleaned saucepan.

Add the cream and some freshly grated nutmeg, check the seasonings and heat until almost boiling but do not boil. Serve garnished with chopped parsley and chopped raw cauliflower.

Serves 6.

Curried Cauliflower Soup

A prize winner! Ideal for lunch or for a light evening meal.

½ medium cauliflower
1 green or red pepper
2 medium onions
2 tablespoons butter
2 teaspoons curry powder
3 cups chicken stock
2 tablespoons pea flour or cornflour
2 cups milk
fresh parsley

Cut cauliflower into small flowerets. Chop the pepper and onions fairly finely. Gently fry the vegetables in butter for about 10 minutes, without browning. Stir in the curry powder and add the chicken stock. Cover and simmer for about 25 minutes. Mix pea flour (much more flavoursome in soups than ordinary flour and available at health food shops) with a little milk and slowly stir into soup. Add remainder of milk and salt to taste. Simmer for a further 10 minutes. Just before serving add a handful of chopped parsley. Serve with fresh rye bread.
Serves 6.

Choko Soup

3 medium chokos
1 medium onion
1 medium potato
2½ cups chicken stock
½ cup cream
½ cup milk
1 tablespoon butter
salt and white pepper
grated nutmeg
parsley or chives to garnish

Peel the chokos under running water (to remove the sticky juice under the skin). Remove the seed and cut into chunks. Peel the onion and potato and chop coarsely. Place the vegetables in a saucepan with the chicken stock and simmer until tender.

Put through a blender and return the purée to the saucepan. Add the cream, milk and butter and season well with salt, white pepper and freshly ground nutmeg. Bring to boiling point, but do not boil, and serve garnished with chopped parsley or snipped chives.

Serves 6.

Corn Chowder

450 g can cream-style sweet corn
500 g very ripe tomatoes, peeled and chopped
3 small potatoes, cooked and diced
2 tablespoons finely chopped green pepper
1 small onion, finely chopped
½ teaspoon thyme
salt and pepper to taste
½ cup cream

Mix all the vegetables and seasoning together and simmer for about an hour. Allow to cool then refrigerate overnight. When serving, reheat, check the seasoning and add the cream. Do not boil. Serve for lunch, supper or as a first course with cracker biscuits.

Serves 6–8.

Courgette and Spaghetti Soup

An Italian-inspired soup with a refreshing flavour of courgettes.

    6 tablespoons olive oil
    1 large onion
    1 clove garlic
    500 g courgettes
    ½ teaspoon dried basil
    2 peeled tomatoes
    salt and freshly ground black pepper
    4 cups chicken stock
    about 150 g spaghetti

In the olive oil, fry the onion, chopped, with the clove garlic, crushed. Fry until they are soft but not browned. Cut the courgettes into very small cubes and add to the onions. Then add the dried basil or a few chopped fresh basil leaves, the peeled tomatoes, coarsely chopped, some salt and plenty of freshly ground black pepper. Add ¾ cup water and cover and simmer for half an hour.

Up to this point the soup can be made ahead of time. Now add the chicken stock and bring to the boil. Break about a third of a packet of spaghetti into 5 cm pieces and add to the soup. Simmer, covered, until spaghetti is al dente. If the soup is not liquid enough add more chicken stock. Serve at once, with or without brown bread.

Serves 6.

Creamed Corn and Bacon Soup

    2 or 3 rashers bacon
    1 medium onion
    2 tablespoons flour
    1 cup dry white wine
    2 cups milk
    1 medium can cream-style sweet corn
    salt and pepper
    parsley to garnish

In a medium saucepan, gently fry the bacon, chopped. When it is nearly crisp add the onion, finely chopped, and gently fry together until the onion is transparent. Remove from the heat. Add the flour, then stir in the white wine and milk. Return to heat and bring to the boil, stirring often. Add the sweet corn and season to taste with salt and pepper. If too thick add more milk. Garnish heavily with chopped parsley.

Serves 4.

Courgette Bisque

Very thick, very creamy, very smooth and very delicious.

    50 g butter
    1 medium onion
    700 g courgettes
    2½ cups chicken stock
    ¼ teaspoon nutmeg
    1 teaspoon basil
    1 teaspoon salt
    freshly ground black pepper
    1 cup cream

In a saucepan melt the butter, chop the onion finely and fry it gently in the butter until soft but not browned. Slice the courgettes and add to the saucepan together with the chicken stock. Cover, and simmer for about 20 minutes. When courgettes are tender, put through blender and return purée to saucepan. Add nutmeg, salt and pepper and cream. Heat but do not boil. Serve with fresh rye bread.
Serves 6.

Cressida Soup

Not too fattening and equally good hot or cold. The inclusion of yoghurt gives this soup a pleasantly refreshing tang.

    1 small onion, finely chopped
    25 g butter
    4 cups chicken stock
    1 large lettuce
    1 bunch watercress
    salt and pepper
    freshly grated nutmeg
    ½ cup plain yoghurt

Sweat the onion in the butter until soft but not browned. Add stock, lettuce and watercress, both shredded (reserve a little of each) and simmer for 5 minutes or so. Purée the soup in the blender, then reheat and season well with salt and pepper and some nutmeg. Just before serving, and away from the heat, add the yoghurt, and the reserved shredded leaves.
Serves 4.

Esquire Soup

3 large potatoes
1 large onion
1 large stalk celery
3 cups chicken stock
2 cups milk
2 tablespoons butter
2 teaspoons dry mustard
salt
parsley or chervil to garnish

Peel and roughly dice the potatoes and onion. Slice the celery and add vegetables to the chicken stock. Simmer gently until vegetables are tender. Put through blender or mouli or rub through sieve and return purée to the saucepan. Add the milk and butter. Mix the mustard to a smooth paste with a little milk and stir into the soup. Simmer gently for a further few minutes. Add salt to taste. If vegetable stock is used instead of chicken stock this makes an excellent vegetarian soup. Serve piping hot garnished with chopped parsley or chervil and accompanied by water crackers.

Serves 6.

Fijian Eggplant Soup

1 small onion, finely chopped
1 clove garlic, finely chopped
1 tablespoon finely chopped green pepper
1 tablespoon oil
1 large tomato, peeled and chopped
2 cups chicken stock or vegetable water
1 medium eggplant, diced
1 cup coconut cream
salt and freshly ground black pepper
finely chopped green pepper to garnish

Gently fry the onion, garlic and green pepper in the oil until soft but not brown. Add the tomato and stock and bring to the boil. Add the eggplant and cook until just tender. Add the coconut cream, season to taste, and heat through without boiling. Garnish with some finely chopped green pepper.

Serves 4.

Green Velvet Soup

A very beautiful soup that can also be used as a recipe for spinach, silver beet, broccoli, asparagus, celery or cauliflower soup.

700 g mixed greens (spinach, silver beet, celery, broccoli)
fresh herbs (sorrel, comfrey, parsley, tarragon etc.)
1 small onion, coarsely chopped
1 small potato, coarsely chopped
2½ cups chicken stock
2 tablespoons butter
½ cup cream
1 cup milk
¼ teaspoon grated nutmeg
salt and white pepper
lemon slices to garnish

Wash the vegetables, stalks and all, and place in a large saucepan. Add the chicken stock, bring to the boil, cover and cook until vegetables are tender. Put through blender and return purée to the saucepan.

Add butter, cream, milk, nutmeg and salt and pepper to taste. Bring almost to boiling but do not boil. Serve hot garnished with a slice of lemon.

Serves 6.

Jerusalem Artichoke Soup

5 cups chicken stock
500 g Jerusalem artichokes
1 medium onion, chopped
1 stalk celery, finely chopped
chopped tarragon
a little finely grated orange rind
freshly grated nutmeg
salt and pepper
cream
chopped parsley

Put the chicken stock in a saucepan. Wash and scrub well the artichokes — there is no need to scrape them unless the soup is for something very, very special — remove any black ends, roughly chop them and immediately put them in the chicken stock to prevent discolouration. Add the onion, celery, tarragon, orange rind and nutmeg, bring to the boil and simmer gently until artichokes and onion are tender.

Put through blender or mill and return purée to the saucepan. Season to taste with salt and pepper and add cream if desired. Heat through and serve garnished with chopped parsley and, perhaps, bread croutons.

Serves 6.

Kumara Soup

Kumara lovers and most others will enjoy this slightly sweet yet extremely tasty soup.

750 g kumara (sweet potato)
2 large onions
3 cups chicken stock
2 cups milk
¼ teaspoon ground cinnamon, or to taste
salt and pepper
fried onion rings
chopped parsley

Peel and coarsely dice the kumara and peel and thinly slice the onions. Cook them in the chicken stock until tender. Put the stock and vegetables through a blender or sieve. Return purée to the saucepan, add the milk, cinnamon, and pepper and salt to taste. Reheat to blend. Serve garnished with onion rings fried until golden brown, and a little chopped parsley.

Serves 6.

Kumara and Celery Soup

The sweetness of kumara and the tanginess of celery make quite an exciting combination.

    4 medium kumara
    ½ medium head celery
    chicken stock
    salt and white pepper
    1 clove garlic, crushed
    300 ml cream

Peel and chop the kumara and place in a saucepan with enough chicken stock to well cover. Bring to the boil and simmer until almost tender. Add the celery, roughly sliced, and cook a further 5 minutes. Blend the vegetables in a blender or food mill and return the purée to the saucepan. Season with salt and white pepper and add the garlic and cream. If too thick, dilute with extra chicken stock. Heat through and serve garnished with a few celery leaves.
Serves 8–10.

Kumara and Pumpkin Soup

    750 g kumara
    1 kg pumpkin
    1 small onion
    6 cups bacon or chicken stock
    25 g butter
    ground allspice
    ½ cup cream
    salt and white pepper
    chopped parsley or chervil to garnish

Peel the kumara, pumpkin and onion, de-seed the pumpkin and cut the vegetables into chunks. Put in a saucepan together with the bacon stock, cover and simmer until the vegetables are tender. Purée in a blender and return the purée to the saucepan.

Add the butter, a little allspice, the cream and season well with salt and white pepper. Reheat to blend but do not boil. Serve garnished with chopped parsley or chervil.
Serves 8–10.

Leek and Watercress Soup

If served cold, this extremely good soup needs extra seasoning and sharpening with fresh lemon juice.

500 g potatoes
A large bunch watercress
4 cups chicken stock
1 kg leeks
25 g butter
2 tablespoons flour
salt and pepper
½ cup cream

Peel and dice the potatoes. Wash the watercress and chop up half of it. Remove and set aside the leaves from the other half and chop up the stalks. Place the potatoes, chopped watercress and chicken stock in a saucepan. Bring to the boil, cover and simmer for 15 to 20 minutes.

Meanwhile, remove roots and coarse outer leaves from the leeks and shred finely. Wash well, then heat butter in a large saucepan and gently fry the shredded leeks until soft but still bright green. Remove from heat and stir in the flour. When smooth gradually add the strained potato/watercress stock. Bring to the boil, stirring continuously, then add potato and watercress. Cover and simmer for 20 minutes. Purée in a blender.

Return the purée to the rinsed saucepan, and add the remaining watercress leaves and cream, and season to taste. Reheat, but do not boil or cream may separate and watercress lose its colour. Serve in heated bowls garnished with swirls of cream.

Serves 6–8.

Welsh Leek Soup

1 kg leeks
1 large onion
1 medium potato
1 stalk celery
7 cups mutton stock
salt and white pepper
chopped parsley to garnish

Slice the leeks down the middle and wash out all the grit. Slice them finely, along with as much of the green part as possible. Peel and finely chop the onion and potato and finely slice the celery. Put the vegetables in a large saucepan along with the mutton stock, bring to the boil and simmer gently for about an hour or until all vegetables are tender. Purée the soup in a food mill, blender or food processor and return the purée to the saucepan. Add the milk and season well with salt and white pepper. Bring to the boil and serve garnished with chopped parsley.

Serves 6–8.

Cream of Lettuce Soup

Any type of lettuce is suitable for this soup which is an excellent way to use up old, wilted lettuces.

2 large lettuces
25 g butter
1 medium onion, finely chopped
1 tablespoon flour
3½ cups milk
salt and pepper
1 teaspoon arrowroot
3 tablespoons cream
fresh mint, finely chopped
fried bread croutons

Wash the lettuce well, then shred it finely. Melt the butter in a saucepan, add the lettuce and onion, cover tightly and cook very gently for 10 minutes. Remove saucepan from the heat and stir in the flour. Scald the milk, blend it with the lettuce mixture and season it well. Stir until boiling then simmer very gently, with lid half on, for 15 minutes. Purée the soup in the blender. Return the soup to the rinsed-out saucepan, reheat and stir in the arrowroot mixed with the cream.

When serving, sprinkle with plenty of chopped mint and pass the fried croutons separately.

Serves 4–6.

Cream of Mushroom Soup

Elegant yet simply made.

4 tablespoons butter
250 g mushrooms, sliced
1 small onion, sliced
3 tablespoons flour
1 cup chicken stock
1 cup cream
1 cup milk
salt and pepper to taste
½ cup dry white wine

Gently fry the mushrooms and the onion in the butter over a low heat for 10 minutes. Remove from heat. Stir in the flour and mix well. Slowly stir in stock, then add cream and milk and mix well. Return to the heat, and cook slowly, stirring, until well blended and thickened. This process should take at least 10 minutes.

Season to taste with salt and pepper and keep the soup hot until ready to serve. Just before serving add the wine and then quickly almost bring to the boil. Serve garnished with a little chopped parsley or strips of red pepper.

Serves 4.

Okra Soup

This relatively uncommon vegetable makes a very good soup. Note that chicken stock could be used but it is not really necessary.

    500 g okra
    2 onions
    2 tablespoons butter
    2 sprigs thyme
    2 sprigs parsley
    1 bay leaf
    1 small chilli
    500 g tomatoes, peeled and chopped
    10 cups water
    salt and freshly ground black pepper

Wash okra, remove the stems and cut into fine slices. Fry the finely chopped onion in the butter, add the herbs and the peeled and chopped tomatoes, stir well, and simmer for 10 minutes. Add the okra, stir for a few minutes, then add the hot water and season with salt and pepper. Simmer 1½ hours then check the seasonings, making sure there is plenty of pepper. Serve with fried croutons.

Serves 8.

Minestrone

Not only does this classic Italian soup vary from town to town and from kitchen to kitchen, it also changes from season to season and almost from one day to the next. It is basically a beef stock which is cooked in combination with many vegetables and pastas, with just enough stock to float both. Here is the favourite version.

1 cup dried kidney beans
3 rashers bacon
2 large onions
7 cups beef stock
2 cloves garlic
⅓ cup olive oil
2 potatoes
2 small carrots
½ cup courgettes
½ celery
1 tablespoon dried basil
4 large tomatoes
1 cup shredded cabbage
1½ cups red or white wine
½ cup macaroni or star pasta
salt and pepper
grated lemon rind
parsley
grated parmesan cheese

Soak the dried kidney beans in 2 cups water overnight. In a large saucepan fry the bacon until crisp. Remove the cracklings and reserve them. In the fat remaining in the saucepan gently fry the onions, coarsely chopped, until they are golden. Add the beef stock to the onions, add the soaked and drained beans together with the crushed cloves of garlic. Simmer beans gently for about an hour or until cooked.

In another saucepan heat the olive oil and add the potatoes, peeled and diced, the carrots, scraped and diced, the courgettes, sliced, the celery including some of the leaves, chopped, and the dried basil. Cook the vegetables for a few minutes, stir in the tomatoes, peeled and seeded, and the shredded cabbage. Mix well.

Add the vegetables to the beans and cook over medium heat for 15 minutes. Stir in the wine and the macaroni or star-shaped pasta and cook a further 15 minutes. Season the soup with salt and pepper to taste and sprinkle it with a mixture of grated lemon rind and chopped parsley.

Serve with grated parmesan cheese.

Serves 10–12.

French Onion Soup

French onion soup evokes Paris in its most romantic mood. It is a wonderful late-night or winter soup, warming and filling. There are many versions of this soup, both simple and elaborate. Here is a favourite.

French bread
butter
grated parmesan cheese
5 cups thinly sliced onions
5 tablespoons butter
1 tablespoon oil
1 teaspoon flour
1 teaspoon Dijon mustard
black pepper
6 cups beef stock
1 cup dry sherry
salt
1/3 cup grated mild cheddar cheese

Cut six 1½ cm slices French bread, diagonally, spread each with butter and sprinkle with grated parmesan cheese. Toast the slices in a 160°C oven until they are golden brown. Let them cool and arrange them in a bread basket.

In a saucepan, gently fry the sliced onions in 5 tablespoons butter and the oil for 30 to 40 minutes or until onions are soft and golden. Stir in the flour and Dijon mustard, add freshly ground black pepper to taste and cook for a few minutes.

Pour in the beef stock, heated, and the sherry and cook the soup over low heat, stirring, until it comes to the boil. Simmer for 30 minutes. Add salt if necessary.

Transfer the soup to an oven-proof earthenware casserole and sprinkle it with the grated mild cheddar cheese and 1/3 cup grated parmesan cheese. Put the casserole under the grill for 3 or 4 minutes or until the cheese is browned and bubbling. Put a slice of the toasted cheese bread in each bowl or mug and pour the soup on top. It is a good idea to make extra toasted cheese bread and pass it around. It makes a worthy nibble with the soup.

Serves 6.

Italian Onion Soup

2 large onions, sliced
2 tablespoons butter
2 tablespoons flour
6 cups rich beef stock
4 egg yolks, beaten slightly
½ cup grated parmesan cheese
chopped parsley
salt and pepper

Gently fry the onions in the butter until brown. Add the flour, stir, and add a little stock. Blend well, then slowly add the remaining stock, stirring constantly. Simmer for 30 minutes. Mix together the egg yolks, cheese and parsley. Add a little of the hot liquid to make a smooth paste, then add egg mixture to the rest of the soup, stir, season with salt and pepper and serve, garnished with more chopped parsley.
Serves 6.

Parsnip Soup

500 g parsnips
1 tablespoon butter
4 cups beef stock
¼ teaspoon nutmeg
2 cups milk
2 cloves garlic
parsley
croutons

Scrub the parsnips and chop them coarsely. Gently fry them in the butter for about 10 minutes, then add the beef stock and simmer until soft. Put through a blender or sieve. Return the purée to the saucepan and add the freshly grated nutmeg, the milk — or milk and cream — and the garlic, crushed. Reheat to blend and season to taste. Just before serving stir in a handful of chopped parsley. Serve with croutons.
Serves 6.

Hot Pepper Soup

Although made with chilli peppers, this soup is not really hot but has a more tangy flavour.

10–12 hot peppers
1 kg ripe tomatoes
1 onion
2 cups water
3 tablespoons butter
3 tablespoons flour
1½ teaspoons grated lemon rind
salt and black pepper
1 cup cooked brown rice
sour cream
fresh dill or parsley

Pick out an assortment of small and medium-sized hot peppers, red, green or yellow. Wash them, cut them open, and discard all the seeds and pulp, unless you want a very fiery soup. Chop the rest very finely.

In a large saucepan combine the peppers, coarsely chopped tomatoes, finely chopped onion and the water. Bring to the boil and simmer until the vegetables are very tender. Rub the mixture through the sieve — it only takes a few minutes and is much better than blending the tomato pips and skins.

Melt the butter in a small saucepan and stir in the flour to make a roux. Cook a few minutes, stirring constantly. Pour some of the heated soup into the roux, stirring to make a thick sauce. Now pour the sauce back into the soup, and stirring occasionally, continue to simmer for about 10 minutes. Add the lemon rind, salt and black pepper, then stir in the brown rice, reheat and serve.

When serving, garnish each bowl with a large dollop of sour cream and chopped fresh dill or parsley.

Serves 6.

Minted Green Pea Soup

A quick refreshing soup, using a good old New Zealand institution, frozen peas.

500 g frozen minted peas
3 cups chicken stock
1 cup milk
½ cup cream
salt and white pepper
plain croutons

In a saucepan bring the peas to the boil in the chicken stock and simmer until tender. Purée the soup in the blender. Return the soup to the saucepan, add the milk and cream and season well with salt and white pepper. Bring to the boil and serve piping hot. Garnish with plain croutons.

Serves 6.

Peapod Soup

This is really a recipe for those who grow their own peas, for the peapods must be absolutely fresh. Try Sugar Snap peas too.

500 g peapods
1 small lettuce, chopped
1 onion, chopped
1 sprig mint
salt and white pepper
½ cup milk
¼ cup cream
A few cooked peas to garnish

Wash the peapods and put in a saucepan with the lettuce, onion and mint. About two-thirds cover with cold water, add some salt, bring to the boil and simmer, covered, until tender. Put through blender or mill and then through a sieve to remove the pod fibres. Return purée to the saucepan, add the milk and reheat gently. Just before serving stir in the cream. Add a few cooked peas to each serving bowl.

Serves 6–8.

Green Pepper and Onion Soup

    2 large onions
    2 cloves garlic
    2 tablespoons oil
    1 large green pepper
    1 large red pepper
    4 cups chicken stock or water
    2 large tomatoes
    1 cup sliced mushrooms
    salt and pepper

Peel the onions, cut them in half and slice finely. Crush the garlic. Heat the oil in a saucepan and toss the onion and garlic in it until soft but not brown. Remove the cores and seeds from the peppers and cut into small strips. Add to the onion. Add the liquid, bring steadily to the boil and add the tomatoes, peeled and coarsely chopped. Continue cooking until the vegetables are soft. Five minutes before serving time add the mushrooms. Season well. Garnish with fresh herbs or croutons.

Serves 6.

Sour Cream Potato Soup

A heart-and-soul warming cold weather soup.

    25 g butter
    700 g potatoes
    2 medium onions
    1 tablespoon paprika
    5 cups chicken stock
    salt and pepper
    2 cups sour cream
    3 tablespoons chopped parsley
    lemon juice

Melt the butter in a saucepan. Peel the potatoes and cut them into small dice. Finely slice the onions. Stew the potatoes and onions with the paprika in the saucepan for 10 minutes, making sure that they don't catch and burn.

Add the chicken stock, season to taste with salt and white pepper and simmer until the potatoes are just cooked. Add the sour cream, parsley and lemon juice to taste and reheat but do not boil. Check seasonings before serving.

Serves 6–8.

Pistou Soup

Originally from Genoa, this flavoursome soup is now a firm favourite of Nice and the surrounding country.

250 g French beans
4 medium potatoes
3 tomatoes
salt and pepper
100 g vermicelli
grated gruyere cheese

Aillade

3 cloves garlic
handful sweet basil or 1 tablespoon dried basil
1 grilled tomato

Into 6 cups boiling water, put the French beans cut into 3 cm lengths, the potatoes, finely cubed, and the tomatoes, chopped and peeled. Season with salt and pepper and let them cook fairly quickly. When the vegetables are almost cooked, throw in the vermicelli and finish cooking gently.

Have ready the following preparation, known as an *aillade*. In a mortar pound the garlic, sweet basil or dried basil, and the grilled tomato, without the skin or pips. When this paste is thoroughly smooth add 3 tablespoons of the liquid from the soup. Pour the soup into a tureen, stir in the aillade and some grated gruyere cheese.

Serves 6.

Curried Radish Soup

This may sound strange but it is very moreish. Radishes when cooked taste something similar to mild turnip so that small white turnips could be used instead.

500 g radishes
1 teaspoon salt
2 cups chicken stock
1 teaspoon curry powder
1 cup cream
salt and white pepper
chopped parsley or snipped chives to garnish

Wash and coarsely chop the radishes and place in a saucepan with just enough water to cover. Add the salt, bring to the boil and simmer for about 10 minutes or until radishes are tender.

Blend the radishes and liquid in a blender along with the chicken stock and curry powder and return to saucepan. Add the cream and check the seasonings. Reheat but do not boil. Serve garnished with chopped parsley or snipped chives. This soup may successfully be served chilled.

Serves 6.

Pumpkin Soup

There are many, many variations of this wonderful soup. To simplify matters here is the idea for the base and the variations that follow.

Select a medium-sized crown pumpkin. Cut it into segments, scoop out the seeds then peel it. (Good luck with the peeling.) Put it in a large saucepan with some bacon rinds or bacon bones, a large potato, peeled and chopped, several onions, peeled and chopped, and several carrots, peeled and sliced.

Cover with water, bring to the boil and simmer, covered, until all the vegetables are very tender, especially the carrots. Remove the bacon bones then purée the soup in the blender. Season well with salt and white pepper. Now use this as the basis for your pumpkin soup. Either freeze it in batches or keep it in the refrigerator in screw top jars. Always check the seasoning after reheating, and add cream or milk as desired.

Variations
Add a handful of chopped parsley, coriander or chives to the basic soup.
Add a can of shrimps.
Add lots of grated cheese, and stir until melted.
Add some freshly grated nutmeg until it is just barely discernible
    in the finished soup.
Dissolve a little curry powder and stir it into the base soup.
    Definitely add some cream.
Fry some onions until deliciously golden and add to the basic soup.
Simply add some crushed garlic, and some cream too.
Add some finely grated lemon rind.
Stir in some sour cream.
Stir in some yoghurt.
Stir in some puréed peaches.
Add some finely chopped mint.
Add some finely grated fresh ginger.
Add some finely chopped fresh basil.

The King's Pumpkin Soup

Elaborate and elegant, a soup fit for you-know-who.

1 kg pumpkin meat
4½ cups chicken stock
1 medium onion, chopped
6 spring onions, chopped
4 tomatoes, peeled and chopped
300 ml cream
juice of 1 lemon
1 teaspoon curry powder
1 teaspoon brown sugar
salt and freshly ground black pepper
whipped cream to garnish
chopped chives to garnish

Simmer until tender the pumpkin, chicken stock, onion, spring onion and tomatoes. Blend in blender, food processor or mill and return purée to saucepan. Add the cream, lemon juice, curry powder and brown sugar, and season to taste with salt and freshly ground black pepper. Reheat to blend but do not boil.

Serve either hot or chilled, with a blob of whipped cream and a sprinkling of chives in each bowl. Accompany with thin slices of rye bread or perhaps Indian chapattis.

Serves 8.

Silver Beet Soup

This delicious soup can also be made with spinach, Brussels sprouts, broccoli, lettuce or other vegetables.

    500 g silver beet
    2 onions, finely sliced
    50 g butter
    4 cups water or chicken stock
    salt and pepper
    2 cloves garlic, crushed
    finely chopped parsley
    2 eggs, beaten
    sour cream to garnish

Separate the green leaves from the stalks of the silver beet. Cut the green leaves crosswise in 1 cm sections and finely slice the stalks. In a large saucepan, gently fry the onion in the butter, until the onion is transparent, then add the stock along with the silver beet. Season with salt, pepper, garlic and parsley. Simmer about 20 minutes. Beat some of the hot soup into the eggs, then beat this mixture back into the soup. Serve immediately, with a swirl of sour cream in each bowl.
Serves 6.

Greek Spinach and Rice Soup

Excellent as a lunch dish served with crusty bread and red wine.

    olive oil
    2 cloves garlic
    3 or 4 small red chilli peppers
    1 bunch spinach
    ½ cup rice
    4 cups water
    salt

Cover the bottom of a saucepan with olive oil. Crush into it the garlic and chilli peppers. Wash the spinach and break it into salad-sized pieces and add to the saucepan. Cover and gently cook the spinach in its own juice and the oil until tender. Add uncooked and unwashed rice and water. Simmer until the rice is tender, about 10 minutes, then continue simmering a further 5 or 10 minutes. It should be fairly thick. Season with salt to taste.
Serves 4.

Tomato Macaroni Soup

Splendidly tangy, this is an excellent year-round soup.

700 g tomatoes
2 onions
1 tablespoon oil
2 sprigs each thyme and parsley
1 teaspoon sugar
5 cups beef stock
salt and pepper to taste
1 cup uncooked macaroni

In a saucepan, put the tomatoes, chopped, and the onions, peeled and chopped. Add the oil, herbs, sugar and stock. Bring to the boil, cover and simmer for half an hour, or until the onions are soft. Put the soup through a sieve, rubbing through as much of the vegetable as you can. Do not vitamise the soup as it will go milky. Return the soup to the saucepan, season to taste with salt and pepper and then add the macaroni. Cook until the macaroni is just tender. Garnish with chopped parsley.

Serves 6–8.

French Vegetable Soup

An old French lady taught me this soup. It is also ideal for children who dislike vegetables and for invalids too.

3 medium potatoes
½ bunch celery
2 large carrots
1 medium turnip
1 medium onion
3 to 4 cauliflower pieces

Clean and wash all vegetables and cut finely. Put in a large saucepan with some butter or margarine and toss over low heat until well coated and even slightly brown. Fill saucepan with fresh cold water; add salt, bay leaves, mixed herbs and cloves (leave out what is not liked). Boil gently for 1 hour or until vegetables are soft. Put through a mouli or blend in the blender. The soup should be fairly thick. Season well with salt and pepper. Serve hot with frankfurters, cheerios, or croutons or plain toast and crackers.

This soup is ideal for leftovers — sweet corn, peas, beans, tomatoes, pumpkin, mashed or cold potato, kumara . . . but avoid cabbage, swede turnips and beetroot.

Old Fashioned Vegetable Soup or Shin Soup

Thick, hearty and nourishing, and a winter standby for almost every home.

In a large saucepan put a lump of shin of beef and a few bacon or ham bones or brisket bones. Cover well with water and add several chopped onions, some chopped celery, herbs (thyme, parsley, bay leaf, for instance), and some dried beans, lentils or barley. Bring to the boil, cover and simmer for several hours or until meat is falling off the bones. Remove bones, fat and gristle and return soup to the stove.

Now add all sorts of vegetables, old gravies and vegetable waters, and any suitable bits and pieces lurking in the refrigerator. Grated carrot, parsnip, turnip, finely diced beetroot, kumara, pumpkin or potato, chopped silver beet, spinach, cauliflower flowerets, a few peeled and chopped tomatoes, any cold, leftover vegetables, can all be added towards the end of cooking. Season well with salt and pepper. This sort of soup will keep on keeping on if you continually add suitable leftovers to the leftover soup.

Cream of Turnip Soup

It sounds unusual but has a delicious flavour. A sort of variation on the Vichyssoise theme but don't eat it cold. It is much better served as a hot soup.

500 g new young turnips
250 g potatoes
3 medium leeks
25 g butter
salt and freshly ground black pepper
4 cups chicken stock
bouquet garni
1½ cups milk
chopped parsley

Peel the turnips and cut into dice. Blanch the turnips by covering with water, bringing to the boil and draining. This removes some of the strong flavour. Peel the potatoes and dice. Wash the leeks and slice, using some of the green part too. Melt the butter in a saucepan and add the leeks. Cover and gently fry for about 5 minutes without browning. Add the turnip and potato, some salt and pepper, cover and cook gently for a further few minutes. Add the stock and bouquet garni and simmer gently for about 30 minutes until the vegetables are tender. Purée the vegetables in a blender. Return the purée to the saucepan, add the hot milk and check the seasoning. Reheat but do not boil and add some chopped parsley just before serving.

Serves 6.

Watercress Soup

large bunch watercress
1 tablespoon butter
4 cups chicken stock
salt and white pepper
1 egg yolk
½ cup cream
chopped fresh chervil or parsley

Wash the watercress and remove the leaves. The stalks tend to be tough and bitter when cooked. Cook the leaves in the butter until wilted then add the chicken stock. Simmer for half an hour then season to taste. Just before serving add the egg yolk and cream, mixed together. Reheat to blend but do not boil. Serve with hot, brown bread rolls.

Serves 4.

Indonesian Watercress Soup

Unlike most Asian soups, this is one case where the vegetable should be thoroughly cooked and not remain crisp.

100 g lean pork, sliced into small pieces
1 teaspoon cornflour
½ teaspoon brown sugar
1 teaspoon freshly ground black pepper
1 tablespoon soy sauce
peanut oil
2 cm ginger, very thinly sliced
500 g watercress, finely shredded
salt

Mix together the pork, cornflour, sugar, pepper, soy sauce and 1 tablespoon peanut oil. In a saucepan fry the ginger in a little moderately hot oil for a minute. Add 7 cups boiling water, bring back to the boil, add the watercress and simmer 5 minutes. Add the pork mixture, stir well, cover and simmer gently for 15 minutes, until everything is tender. Add salt to taste. Serve piping hot.

Serves 6–8.

SEAFOOD SOUPS

This Bouillabaisse a noble dish is —
A sort of soup, or broth, or brew.
William Makepeace, *The Ballad of Bouillabaisse*

The best soups of many countries are created from seafood. Consider the superb clam chowders of America, the classic Bouillabaisse, Matelote and Bourride of France, New Zealand's unique toheroa and tuatua soups, the Italian Zuppa di Pesce, the Dutch and German eel soups and the Scandinavian fish and herring soups, for example.

Most fish soups are relatively quick soups since fish cooks very quickly and most shellfish simply need to be just heated through or at the most cooked for only a few minutes.

Chowders are usually thick seafood soups with the addition of vegetables. *Bisques* are cream of shellfish soups. When fishermen's soup/stews are served, the fish is often presented on the side and eaten with knife and fork, and the stock eaten with a spoon.

There is one thing wrong with fish soups though, especially those using oily fish: production of the soup can be a very smelly affair indeed. The end result, however, is usually delicate and superb.

There is not the same problem with shellfish, though you must be careful with them. Shellfish are scavengers and will go rotten very quickly and thus become extremely poisonous. Just make sure you know where the shellfish come from, and their age.

To rid live shellfish of most of their sand, simply leave them overnight in a bucket of water to which you have added a good handful of rolled oats or wheatgerm or the like. They will eat the cereal and eject the sand.

There is a host of materials to draw on in the seafood world: the sixty or so varieties of fresh fish, the many fresh shellfish, smoked fish and shellfish and the canned fish and shellfish.

Bouillabaisse

Bouillabaisse is the most famous of the fish-soup-plus-fish dishes and naturally a great number of recipes have been published. Marseille is the top seaport city for Bouillabaisse where such fish as rascasse, chapon rouge and sea perch, all uniquely Mediterranean, are used.

All fish should be straight from the sea and if conger eel is used it should be added live. The liquid used consists of olive oil and water which must be rapidly boiled to ensure amalgamation. Often the fish is served separately, filleted at the table, and the broth is poured over pieces of toast and accompanied by a garlic and red pepper sauce.

Here then is Bouillabaisse — New Zealand style. And superb it is.

2 kg fresh fish (gurnard, mullet, snapper, mackerel, trevally, tuna,
  leatherjacket, etc.) to give about 1 kg flesh
100 g fresh shrimps (i.e. not canned)
1 large onion, chopped
3 large cloves garlic, crushed
3 large tomatoes, peeled and chopped
½ cup leeks, white part only
2 large sprigs parsley
sprig of thyme
sprig of fennel
large piece of orange peel
salt and freshly ground black pepper
good pinch of saffron
¾ cup olive oil
long soft white loaf
chopped parsley

Prepared fish by removing the heads, skinning and filleting. Separate the firm flesh from the soft flesh. Put the heads, tails, bones and trimmings into a saucepan, cover with water and simmer for half an hour to make a fish bouillon.

Chop the vegetables up small and put in a large saucepan with the herbs, orange peel and seasonings. Pour over olive oil and boil furiously for 7–8 minutes. Add firm-fleshed fish chunks first. Strain the fish bouillon into saucepan and boil 5 minutes. Then add the rest of the fish, reserving shrimps. Bring to the boil, and simmer for a few minutes until fish is cooked. Total cooking time will be up to 15 minutes. Add shrimps and chopped parsley. To serve, put slices of bread into a large tureen, cover with the fish pieces and pour the soup over, removing the herbs and orange peel. Garnish with chopped parsley. Essentially this is more a stew than a soup. Just enough liquid is needed to keep it sloppy.

Serves 6–8.

Chinese Crab Soup

4 tablespoons oil
3 slices fresh ginger
½ cup onion, finely chopped
½ cup crab meat
¼ teaspoon salt
1 tablespoon sherry
4 cups chicken stock
2 egg whites
¼ cup cream
2 teaspoons cornflour
paprika

Warm the oil slightly. Add the fresh ginger and the onion. Gently fry for about 1 minute. Add the crab meat, canned or fresh, the salt and the sherry. Continue to cook 1 minute. Add the chicken stock and bring to the boil. Remove the ginger. Combine the egg whites, lightly beaten, with the cream, add the cornflour mixed with 2 tablespoons cold water, and gradually add to the crab mixture, stirring constantly. Simmer gently about 1 minute and serve at once, garnished with paprika.

Serves 4.

Manhattan Clam Chowder

Tuatua, pipis or cockles can be substituted for clams in this excellent bacon and tomato flavoured chowder.

250 g bacon, finely chopped
4 medium onions, finely chopped
4 carrots, finely diced
2 stalks celery, finely sliced
2 tablespoons chopped parsley
750 g tomatoes, peeled and chopped
2½ cups shellfish in liquor
2 teaspoons salt
freshly ground black pepper
1½ teaspoons dried thyme
1 bay leaf
3 medium potatoes, finely diced

Fry the bacon in a large saucepan until almost crisp. Add the onions and cook until limp. Add the carrots, celery and parsley and cook over low heat for about 5 minutes. Add the tomatoes or if using canned tomatoes, drain them, putting the liquid in a measuring cup, and add the pulp to the saucepan. Drain any liquid from the shellfish and add to the tomato liquid. Add enough water to make up 6 cups of liquid and pour into saucepan. Season with the salt, plenty of freshly ground black pepper, thyme, bay leaf, and bring to the boil. Simmer gently for 40 minutes, then add the potatoes and cook a further 20 minutes. Finally, add the chopped shellfish and simmer 15 minutes longer. Serve immediately with large water crackers.

Serves 8.

New England Clam Chowder

The most famous of American chowders is Clam chowder, with its two essential ingredients clams and salt pork or bacon. But 'essential' is a prickly word. Every New Englander has his own version of what is essential to Clam chowder. The most notable heresy is Manhattan Clam chowder which calls for water rather than milk — and tomatoes. Both versions are excellent however, and if clams are not available, local shellfish like cockles, tuatuas or pipis can be substituted.

2½ cups shellfish with liquor
3 cups water
2 rashers bacon, chopped
1 medium onion, halved and sliced
3 medium potatoes, cut into small cubes
3 tablespoons butter
1 cup milk
¾ cup cream
salt and white pepper

Combine the shellfish, liquor and water and bring to the boil. Drain, reserving the broth. When cool enough to handle, either mince or finely chop the shellfish. Set all aside. In a large saucepan, fry the bacon until nearly crisp and then stir in the onion and cook until limp but not brown. Add the shellfish broth and potatoes and cook until potatoes are tender. Stir in the butter, milk, cream and shellfish and season to taste. Heat but do not boil and pour immediately into warmed soup bowls. Serve with cracker biscuits.

Serves 6–8.

Prince Edward Island Clam Chowder

During the winter, heavy snowstorms isolate many residents of this Canadian maritime province for months, and even when spring comes, the red clay roads are impassable until dry weather. Canned goods are practical necessities for people in remote areas and this chowder was born in the tin. Even the clams are canned but the unusual flavour is dependent upon canned evaporated milk, so this should be retained even when fresh ingredients are substituted. Other shellfish can be used instead of clams. (To make Prince Edward Island Corn chowder, substitute a large can of cream-style sweet corn for the clams.)

50 g butter
½ cup finely chopped onion
2 tins baby clams, each tin about 300 g
250 tin baby potatoes
310 g tin condensed celery soup
400 g tin unsweetened condensed evaporated milk
salt and while pepper

In a saucepan, melt the butter and gently fry the onion until just transparent. Add the clams (and juice), potatoes and celery soup. Bring to the boil and add the evaporated milk. Reduce heat and slowly heat the soup until almost boiling. Do not let it boil or the milk will curdle. Serve with wholewheat bread or crackers and pickled beets.

Serves 4.

Crayfish Bisque

Sheer luxury.

750 g crayfish shells
2½ cups chicken or fish stock
1 sliced onion
4 stalks celery with leaves, sliced
2 whole cloves
1 bay leaf
6 peppercorns
50 g butter
¼ cup flour
3 cups heated milk
¼ teaspoon nutmeg
1½ cups diced crayfish meat
1 cup cream
salt and white pepper
chopped parsley
paprika

Crush the crayfish shells — put them in a plastic bag and give them hell with a rolling pin — and place in a saucepan with the stock, onion, celery, cloves, bay leaf and peppercorns. Bring to the boil and simmer for 30 minutes. Strain the stock. In another saucepan melt the butter and add the flour, stir until blended then gradually add the milk. When the sauce is smooth and blended add the nutmeg, stock and crayfish meat. Simmer 5 minutes, then add the cream and season to taste with salt and white pepper. Serve at once, garnished with chopped parsley and paprika.
Serves 8.

Dutch Eel Soup

The great national dish of Holland, simple and satisfying.

500 g fresh eel, cleaned and sliced
7 cups salted water
50 g capers
small bunch parsley
3 tablespoons butter
3 tablespoons flour
salt and pepper

In a saucepan combine the eel and salted water and cook the eel until tender, about 25–35 minutes. Remove eel from water and when cool enough to handle remove the flesh from the bones. Add the capers and parsley to the stock and bring to the boil.

Mix the softened butter and the flour together to make a *beurre manie*, and when smooth add bit by bit to the boiling soup. Season with salt and white pepper and simmer 10 minutes. Strain the soup into a heated tureen and add the pieces of cooked eel.

Serves 6.

Fish Chowder

Smooth and delicious, this chowder-like soup is suitable for any white fish, snapper, tarakihi, moki or blue cod, for example.

1 kg snapper fillets or 1 whole fish
1 carrot, thinly sliced
2 stalks celery, thinly sliced
2 sprigs parsley
1 bay leaf
2 cloves
6 whole peppercorns
water to cover
4 tablespoons butter
3 tablespoons flour
600 ml milk
salt and white pepper
chopped parsley

In a saucepan place the fish, vegetables, parsley, bay leaf, cloves and peppercorns and cover with water. Bring to the boil and simmer until fish is just cooked. Allow to cool then strain, reserving the stock. Flake the fish, discarding the vegetables and any skin and bones.

In the cleaned saucepan, melt the butter, stir in the flour and cook a few minutes. Gradually add the stock and milk and bring to the boil, stirring often. Add salt and pepper to taste. Add the flaked fish and plenty of finely chopped parsley. Heat through and serve with fresh brown bread.

Serves 8–10.

Fish and Macaroni Chowder

500 g green beans, fresh or frozen
500 g carrots
1 cup thinly sliced celery
1 small onion, thinly sliced
¼ cup butter
500 g snapper fillets or other favourite fish
2½ teaspoons salt
½ teaspoon freshly ground black pepper
½ teaspoon dried thyme
¼ teaspoon dried marjoram
1 clove garlic, crushed
1 bay leaf
250 g macaroni
2 cups milk

Cook the sliced beans and the sliced carrots separately in a little lightly salted water until barely tender. Drain and reserve the water. In a large saucepan cook the celery and onion in the butter for several minutes. Add the fish, cut into cubes, and the seasonings.

Add enough water to the vegetable liquids to make 7½ cups and add to the saucepan. Bring to the boil, cover and simmer 15 minutes. Stir in the uncooked macaroni and simmer, covered, stirring occasionally, for 10 minutes or until the macaroni is just cooked. Add the milk and vegetables and heat. Serve with crusty French bread.

Serves 6–8.

Norwegian Fish Soup

Serve either as a first course or add more fish and vegetables and serve as a main course.

Stock

1 fish head (weighing at least 1 kg)
1 litre water
½ parsnip, chopped
1 carrot, chopped
1 potato, chopped
1 onion, chopped
1 teaspoon salt
½ teaspoon celery seed
1 bay leaf
7 whole black peppercorns

Soup

2 carrots, chopped
1 parsnip, chopped
1 leek, chopped
500 g fish fillets
2 cups milk
1 glass white wine
2 large egg yolks
6 tablespoons sour cream
salt
3 tablespoons chopped parsley

Combine the ingredients for the stock in a big saucepan. Bring to the boil and simmer for 40 minutes. Strain the stock through a sieve, pressing down the fish and vegetables to extract all the juices before discarding them. Return the stock to a clean saucepan. Add the vegetables, fish fillets, milk and white wine and simmer for 10 minutes. Lift out the fish and set aside.

Beat egg yolks and add ½ cup soup. Pour this back into the soup, beating continuously at the same time. Separate fish into flakes and add this and sour cream to the soup. Reheat but do not boil. Check seasoning. Serve sprinkled with the parsley.

Serves 6.

Mussel Chowder

A smooth and richly flavoured soup-stew. Chopped raw tuatua, toheroa, pipis or oysters could be substituted for the mussels.

100 g streaky bacon
1 large onion, chopped
1 stalk celery, chopped
1 green pepper, cored, seeded and chopped
2 medium potatoes, cubed
1 bay leaf
2 cups water
salt and pepper
5 tablespoons flour
600 ml milk
400 g cooked mussels, chopped
chopped parsley

Remove the rind and cut the bacon into dice. Gently fry in a dry saucepan, stirring, until it starts to brown. Add the onion and celery and cook until golden. Add the green pepper, potatoes, bay leaf, water, and salt and pepper. Bring to the boil and simmer until potatoes are tender. Mix the flour with ½ cup of the milk and stir into the chowder. Stir until boiling. Add the rest of the milk and the mussels and simmer for 4 to 5 minutes. Serve garnished with chopped parsley.

Serves 4–6.

Mussels a la Mariniere

This classic French way with mussels can equally successfully be applied to other shellfish such as tuatuas, toheroas or cockles. Make sure they contain a minimum of sand though.

```
1 cup dry white wine
3 shallots or spring onions, chopped
4 sprigs parsley
½ bay leaf
½ teaspoon thyme
freshly ground black pepper
3 tablespoons butter
1.5 kg mussels, scrubbed and bearded
¼ cup chopped parsley
```

Combine the wine, shallots, parsley sprigs, bay leaf, thyme, black pepper and butter in a large saucepan. Bring to the boil and simmer for about 3 minutes. Add the mussels to the saucepan, cover and cook quickly over high heat. Occasionally shake the saucepan up and down, holding the lid tightly in place. This will redistribute the mussels so they will cook evenly. Cook 5 or 10 minutes or until the mussels are opened. Discard any mussels that do not open. Spoon the mussels (in their shells) into soup bowls. Spoon the liquid over the mussels and sprinkle with the chopped parsley. Eat with fork and soup spoon. Serve with hot, buttered French bread rubbed with garlic.

Serves about 4.

Oyster Soup

```
1 tablespoon butter
1 tablespoon flour
salt and white pepper
mace
2½ cups milk
oyster liquor
18 oysters, chopped
1 teaspoon lemon juice
```

In a saucepan melt the butter and stir in the flour, add the seasonings and cook, stirring for a minute. Gradually add the milk and oyster liquor, stirring, and heat until almost boiling. Add the chopped oysters and lemon juice and heat for a minute. Serve immediately with melba toast.

Serves 4.

Salmon Soup

An excellent way of combining soup and fish courses to make an interesting and different opening to a dinner party.

1 small onion
3 tablespoons butter
3 tablespoons flour
1 teaspoon paprika
2 cups milk
2 cups chicken stock
salt to taste
250 g can salmon
1 teaspoon lemon juice

Chop the onion finely and gently fry in the butter in a heavy saucepan, until tender but not brown. Blend in the flour and paprika and stir in milk and stock. Keep stirring constantly until smooth and boiling. Season with salt. Remove all skin and large bone from salmon and mash to a fine purée. Sprinkle with lemon juice and stir into soup. Lightly mix with a wire whisk then turn into double boiler or stand saucepan in larger pan of hot water until required. Must be served very hot but do not allow to boil while waiting. Garnish with paprika or chopped parsley if desired.
Serves 4–6.

Paua Soup

A strongly flavoured soup for paua lovers and those who like strong seafood flavours.

700 g paua or abalone, minced
1 small onion, minced
1.25 litres milk
2 tablespoons flour
salt and white pepper to taste
chopped parsley or chives

Mince paua and onion. Boil with one half of the milk for 30 minutes, strain. Mix the flour with some of the other half of the milk. Then add with the rest and heat slowly until it thickens. Season and serve with chopped parsley or chives. Note that if the flavour is too strong, more milk can be added.
Serves 6–8.

Pipi Soup

As in most shellfish soups, other shellfish can be substituted for the pipis.

2 cups minced pipis
50 g butter
4 tablespoons flour
1 clove garlic, crushed
1 teaspoon curry powder
2½ cups milk
2½ cups water and juices
salt and white pepper
chopped parsley

Mince the pipis and set aside, reserving any juices for the sauce. In a saucepan melt the butter, add the flour, garlic and curry powder and stir until smooth. Remove from heat and add the milk, water and juices. Return to heat and heat slowly, stirring, until the soup is smooth and thickened. Just before serving, add the minced pipis and season with salt and white pepper. Serve garnished with chopped parsley.

Serves 6.

Chilled Prawn Bisque

A rich cream soup that can successfully be served hot as well.

200 g shelled prawns, chopped
1 onion, finely chopped
25 g butter
1 kg tomatoes or the equivalent canned tomatoes
1 medium red pepper, chopped
1 tablespoon tomato paste
5 cups chicken stock
arrowroot
½ cup cream

Cook the onion in the butter until soft but not browned, then add the tomatoes, skinned, cut in half with the seeds squeezed out. Cover the saucepan and slowly cook the vegetables to a pulp. Add the red pepper, the tomato paste and the stock. Simmer for about 10 minutes. Then add the prawns and purée the soup in a blender. Thicken it lightly with arrowroot, and chill.

Whip the cream and stir into the soup just before serving. If wished the soup can be garnished with extra prawns and a sprig of watercress.

Serves 6.

Oyster Bisque

Oystery, thickish and absolutely delicious.

1 tablespoon butter
1 tablespoon flour
4 cups milk, scalded
½ cup finely chopped celery
1 small green pepper, seeded and minced
salt and white pepper
24 oysters (approx) minced, with liquid included
Worcestershire sauce

Melt the butter in a saucepan and blend in the flour. Gradually whisk in the milk and bring the mixture to the boil, stirring constantly. Add the celery, green pepper, salt and pepper. Add the minced oysters and heat through, but do not boil. Add Worcestershire sauce to taste.

Serves 4–6.

Scallop Cream Soup

Rich and extravagant and absolutely gorgeous.

3 cups milk
1 cup cream
2 tablespoons butter
2 teaspoons sugar
1 teaspoons Worcestershire sauce
1½ teaspoons salt
¼ teaspoon white pepper
500 g scallops
paprika and chopped parsley to garnish

In the top part of a large double boiler, over boiling water, heat the first 7 ingredients. Mince the scallops and add to the milk mixture. Cook for 5 minutes only. Serve sprinkled with paprika and chopped parsley.

Serves 6.

Seafood Chowder

A deliciously thick shellfish soup which is a meal in itself. Pipis, tuatuas, mussels or cockles can all be successfully substituted for the clams.

6 tablespoons butter
6 tablespoons flour
900 ml milk
4 tablespoons finely sliced spring onions
1 heaped teaspoon curry powder
1 can clams, finely minced
125 g scallops
125 g prawns
¾ cup dry white wine
salt and freshly ground black pepper
finely chopped parsley

In a saucepan melt the butter and blend in the flour. Cook the roux for a few minutes. Gradually add the hot milk, stirring continuously. Add the spring onions and the curry powder. Simmer, stirring, until the sauce is thickened and well blended. Add the minced clams and juice, halved scallops and whole prawns, and cook for a few minutes. Just before serving add the white wine and season to taste with salt and freshly ground black pepper. Heat through and serve immediately in large bowls. Sprinkle with chopped parsley.

Serves 4.

Tivoli Chowder

A fish and vegetable chowder in a creamy smooth sauce. With crusty bread or bread rolls it makes a meal in itself.

500 g any white fish (snapper, tarakihi, etc.)
½ cup white wine
50 g butter
1 onion, sliced
2 stalks celery, sliced
1 carrot, sliced
2 cups chicken stock
½ cup peas
½ cup whole kernel corn
3 tablespoons flour
1 cup milk
½ teaspoon thyme
salt and white pepper
chopped parsley or dill to garnish

Put fish in saucepan with the wine, cover and cook over low heat until fish flakes easily. Drain, reserving the liquid. When the fish is cool enough to handle, flake it, discarding all bone and skin.

In another saucepan melt 25 g of the butter, add the onion, celery and carrot, cook for a few minutes then add the chicken stock. Cover and simmer until vegetables are tender, about 10 minutes, then add the peas and corn and cook a further minute.

In the saucepan in which the fish was cooked, melt the other 25 g butter, add the flour then stir in milk, add the thyme and bring to the boil, stirring constantly. Add the fish stock and vegetable liquid, and bring to the boil, again stirring constantly. Add the vegetables and the flaked fish and adjust the seasoning. Heat thoroughly. Garnish with chopped fresh parsley or dill.

Serves 4–6.

Indonesian Shrimp Soup

2 cloves garlic, peeled and left whole
1 small slice fresh ginger
1 tablespoon peanut oil
¾ cup shrimps
½ teaspoon freshly ground black pepper
salt
100 g egg noodles
1 small leek, sliced finely

Lightly brown the garlic and ginger in the peanut oil. Add 4 cups boiling water, put on high heat and immediately add the shrimps, pepper and a little salt. Cook for 5 minutes. Add the noodles, turn heat to low and simmer for about 15 minutes. Add the leek 5 minutes before serving time. Before serving remove the garlic, and check the seasoning.

Serves 4.

Smoked Fish Chowder

A hearty, tasty, thick, family favourite.

1 medium smoked fish
2 cups diced potatoes
½ cup sliced celery
¾ cup finely chopped onion
4 tablespoons butter
4 tablespoons flour
1 teaspoon salt
½ teaspoon dry mustard
½ teaspoon Worcestershire sauce
2 cups milk
250 g grated medium cheddar cheese
chopped parsley
2–3 tomatoes

Shred the smoked fish. In 2½ cups boiling salted water, simmer the potatoes, celery and onion, until tender. Melt the butter in a large saucepan. Combine with the flour and add the salt, dry mustard, Worcestershire sauce and milk. Stir until thickened, then add the grated cheese and stir over low heat until melted.

Add the drained vegetables, some chopped parsley and the sliced, peeled tomatoes. Add the shredded fish and heat through. If the chowder is too thick, dilute with more milk — or some of the vegetable water — until the required consistency.

Serves 4.

Toheroa Soup

Tuatua or pipis can be substituted in this classic New Zealand soup.

Mince raw toheroas with a little onion and parsley. Put in a saucepan with 2 cups water to each cup of toheroas. Simmer gently until the toheroas are soft, about half an hour. Strain through a coarse sieve, pushing through as much liquid as possible. Return stock to the saucepan and add milk to taste and thicken with pea flour or arrowroot mixed with a little water. Add pepper and salt to taste and a knob of butter. Just before serving add a little freshly grated nutmeg. One cup toheroas makes enough soup to serve 4.

Tuatua Soup

Pipis or other shellfish can be substituted for tuatua in this very delicious soup.

2 cups shelled tuatuas
2 cloves garlic
1 medium onion
1 stalk celery
1 bay leaf
¼ teaspoon dried thyme
¼ teaspoon freshly grated nutmeg
4 cups stock and/or water
rind of 1 lemon
50 g butter
3 tablespoons flour
salt and white pepper
½ cup cream

Steam open the tuatua, cool and remove the flesh, reserving the juices. Measure the prepared shellfish and mince along with the garlic, onion, celery and bay leaf. Place in a saucepan along with the thyme, nutmeg, and the juices from the tuatuas made up to 4 cups liquid with water. Add the peeled lemon rind and simmer for 20 minutes. Strain through a sieve, pressing all the liquid from the mixture. Rinse the saucepan, melt the butter in it then stir in the flour and cook a few minutes. Gradually add the liquid, stirring, taking care not to add any sand. Slowly bring to the boil. Just before serving, reheat and add the cream. Do not boil. Serve with a swirl of cream in each bowl.

Serves 4–6.

Tuna and Celery Soup

4 tablespoons butter
⅓ cup flour
4 cups chicken stock
185 g can tuna
3 stalks celery
3 spring onions
salt and white pepper
⅓ cup cream

Melt the butter in a saucepan, stir in the flour and cook for 1 minute. Gradually add the chicken stock, bring to the boil stirring, and cook until smooth and thickened. Add undrained tuna, the celery, finely sliced on the angle, the spring onions finely sliced, and season to taste with salt and white pepper. Bring to the boil, cover and simmer for 10 minutes. Stir in cream and heat gently. Serve with melba toast. Garnish with celery leaves.

Serves 4–6.

Tuna and Corn Chowder

So quick and easy and being basically made from cans this soup is ideal for unexpected feeding or entertaining.

1 tablespoon butter
1 tablespoon flour
2 cups milk
1 chicken stock cube
1 can whole kernel sweet corn
1 can tuna
salt and white pepper
dry sherry

Melt the butter, add the flour and cook for a few minutes, stirring. Add the milk and chicken stock cube and simmer, stirring often, until the sauce is thickened. Stir in the sweet corn and bring to the boil. Add the shredded tuna and heat through. Correct the seasoning and serve immediately. Just before serving add a little dry sherry. And if the chowder is too thick, dilute with extra milk.

Serves 4.

CHILLED SOUPS

While we send for the napkin the soup gets cold,
While the bonnet is trimming the face grows old,
When we've matched our buttons the pattern is sold,
And everything comes too late — too late.
Fitzhugh Ludlow, *Too Late*

There is a type of remark which is completely unamusing and can happen when you serve a brilliant chilled soup. It is from some so-called wit who declares: 'You've forgotten to heat the soup!' We can do without such ignorance; to prevent this type of remark put a block of ice in the soup — no one likes to state the obvious. A chilled soup is not simply your normal soup served chilled — it is a soup that has been designed to be served chilled, though some can be served hot fairly successfully.

Chilled soups are not only pleasantly cooling and refreshing in hotter weather but from the cook's point of view they are excellent to serve because they must be prepared in advance and refrigerated until ready to use, thus preventing another last-minute panic.

The most popular of these soups come from the warmer European climates, though chilled soups have crept around the world.

Generally it is better to thicken a chilled soup with cream rather than a flour, as the chilled cream should give the soup a heavy enough consistency.

A nice extra touch is to chill the bowls as well as the soup. But perhaps you are fortunate to have access to those double dishes designed for cold soups, where you put cracked ice in the bottom glass dish and the chilled soup in the top one. They are very elegant indeed.

For more chilled soup recipes, refer to the chapter on Fruit Soups. Many of those are also chilled. The chapters on Vegetable Soups and Dried Bean Soups offer a few soups which can be chilled also.

Avocado and Garlic Soup

Sheer ambrosia.

1 large avocado
1½ cups chicken stock, cold
juice of 1 lime or lemon
1 clove garlic, chopped
½ cup cream
salt and pepper

Into a blender scoop out the flesh of the avocado including as much of the dark green flesh as possible, for colour as well as economics. Add the remaining ingredients and blend until smooth. Check the seasoning and chill until ready to use. Garnish with chopped parsley and fresh coriander leaves.
Serves 2.

Chilled Carrot and Tomato Soup

Totally raw and totally refreshing.

1 kg tomatoes
1 kg young carrots
juice and grated rind of 1 large orange
salt and sugar
1 cup yoghurt

Peel the carrots and tomatoes, chop them and purée them with the orange juice and grated rind in a blender. (If the carrots are old and coarse the purée will be stringy, so strain it and return some of the pulp to the liquid.) Season with salt and sugar to taste. Chill well and serve with plenty of yoghurt swirled into each bowl.
Serves 6–8.

Iced Carrot and Orange Soup

350 g carrots
2 onions
1 leek
¼ cup oil
1 teaspoon grated orange rind
¼ cup orange juice
5 cups vegetable stock
1 clove garlic
salt
pinch cayenne
¼ teaspoon freshly ground black pepper
1 teaspoon sugar
mint

Peel the carrots and onions and wash the leek well. Chop the vegetables coarsely.
Heat the oil in a saucepan and cook the vegetables until soft but not coloured.
Add the orange rind, juice, stock, crushed garlic and seasonings. Bring to the boil,
lower heat and simmer for 45 minutes until the vegetables are tender. Purée in a
blender or press through a fine sieve. Chill for several hours. Garnish with sprigs
of mint.
Serves 4–6.

Chinese Cucumber Soup

2 small cucumbers
2 small onions
5 cups chicken stock
salt and white pepper
2 teaspoons lemon juice
4 teaspoons cornflour

Peel and thinly slice the cucumbers and onions. Bring the stock to the boil. Add
the cucumber and onion slices, bring back to the boil and simmer gently for
about 5 minutes or until the vegetables are crisp-tender. Season to taste and add
the lemon juice. Mix cornflour with a little cold water, stir into the soup and
simmer for 3 minutes, stirring constantly. Cool, then refrigerate until ready to
use. Serve garnished with a very thin slice of unpeeled cucumber and accompany
with plain crackers.
Serves 6.

Lebanese Cucumber and Prawn Soup

An excellent starter to a dinner party and such a change from the inevitable prawn cocktail or indifferent cold cucumber soup.

1 medium cucumber, peeled and diced
2 small cans prawns or shrimps
2 cloves garlic, crushed
½ cup beef stock
250 g sour cream
½ teaspoon sugar
juice of ½ lemon
salt and white pepper to taste
paprika to garnish

In a bowl combine all ingredients except the paprika. Chill thoroughly — at least 2 hours. Serve in small bowls garnished with paprika.
Serves 6.

Cucumber and Yoghurt Soup

Very simple yet very elegant.

1 large cucumber
1 cup cream
1 cup milk
1 chicken stock cube or 1 teaspoon chicken stock powder
2 tablespoons lemon juice
500 g plain yoghurt
salt and white pepper
½ cup whipped cream

In a blender, liquidise the cucumber, cream, milk and chicken stock together. Put in a large bowl and stir in the lemon juice and yoghurt. Taste for seasoning. Chill. Just before serving stir in the whipped cream. Garnish with thin slices of cucumber.
Serves 4.

Chilled Curry Soup

1 large onion
1 green apple
1 large banana
50 g butter
3 tablespoons curry powder
5 cups chicken stock
6 cardamom pods
1 tablespoon lemon juice
1 tablespoon Indian mango chutney
salt to taste

Finely chop the onion. Peel, core and finely chop the apple. Peel and slice the banana. Gently fry the onion and apple in the butter in a large covered saucepan for 5 minutes, until soft and golden. Add the banana and cook gently for 5 minutes, stirring with a wooden spoon. Stir in the curry powder and cook 1 minute, then stir in the chicken stock.

Shell the cardamom pods, crush the black seeds and add to the soup with the lemon juice and chutney. Simmer 20 minutes. Add salt to taste. Stir in more curry for a hotter soup. Cool then chill thoroughly before serving.

Serves 6–8.

Iced Curry Soup with Apricot Cream

Delightfully refreshing with a delicious, sweet-curry flavour.

100 g butter
2 medium onions, coarsely chopped
3 stalks celery, chopped
2 tablespoons flour
1 teaspoon curry powder
2 apples, peeled and chopped
5 cups chicken stock
1 bay leaf

Cook the onions and celery in the butter until soft, but not brown. Add the flour and curry powder, stir well and cook for a few minutes. Transfer the mixture to a blender. Add the raw apple and 1 cup stock. Blend until smooth. Return the purée to the saucepan and add the remaining stock. Add the bay leaf. Bring to the boil. Remove the bay leaf and chill. Swirl in the apricot cream when serving.
Serves 6–8.

Apricot Cream

1 cup port
½ cup apricot purée or jam
2 teaspoons curry powder
½ cup slightly whipped cream

In a saucepan, reduce the port by about half. Add the apricot purée and curry powder and cook for 5 minutes over gentle heat. Allow to cook then stir in the cream. Chill.

Cream of Curry Soup

So simple to make, yet this tastes as if hours have gone into its preparation. Perfect in warm weather.

    5 cups milk
    2 egg yolks
    2 tablespoons curry powder
    salt and white pepper to taste
    desiccated coconut

Heat the milk to almost boiling in a saucepan. Beat the egg yolks well and pour the hot milk over them. Beat again, then return to saucepan and heat, stirring, for a few minutes. Mix the curry powder with a little of the milk, then stir into the soup. Season with salt and white pepper. Allow to cool, then refrigerate until very cold. Serve garnished with a little coconut.

Serves 4.

Cold Curried Cream of Eggplant Soup

Smooth and delightful.

    600 g eggplant
    ½ cup chopped onion
    50 g butter
    1 tablespoon curry powder
    4 cups chicken stock
    ¾ cup cream
    salt and white pepper
    finely chopped parsley

Trim and peel the eggplant and cut it into small cubes. In a saucepan gently fry the onion in the butter until soft. Stir in the curry powder and cook over moderate heat, stirring, for 2 minutes. Add the eggplant and the chicken stock, bring to the boil and simmer for about 45 minutes, or until the eggplant is very soft.

Blend the mixture in batches, then strain the purée through a fine sieve, to remove the seeds, etc. to make a very smooth soup. Add the cream and salt and white pepper to taste. Let the soup cool, then chill it for at least 3 hours. Serve garnished with finely chopped parsley.

Serves 4–6.

Gazpacho

The nicest, easiest, tastiest and most beautiful summer soup.

    2 large tomatoes, peeled
    1 cucumber, peeled
    1 green pepper, cored and seeded
    ½ cup olive oil
    garlic
    4 slices white bread
    ¼ cup white wine vinegar
    3 spring onions
    salt and pepper and tabasco sauce

Chop the vegetables and bread very finely and mix with the other ingredients. Alternatively, put everything in the blender and purée. Make sure the soup is well seasoned. Chill thoroughly before serving. Serve everyone a bowl of soup and have a large platter of garnishes to pass around. Finely chop all or some of the following, with an eye for colour (croutons are a must): cucumbers, tomato, green pepper, onion, celery, bread croutons fried in olive oil.
Serves 4.

Summer Pea Soup

    2½ cups peas
    1 large potato, sliced
    2 sprigs mint, chopped
    1 lettuce, broken into pieces
    3 cups chicken stock
    1 cup milk or cream
    juice of 1 small lemon
    salt and freshly ground black pepper
    extra mint to garnish

In a saucepan combine the peas, potato, mint, lettuce, and the chicken stock. Cover and simmer for about 15 minutes or until the vegetables are tender. Put through a blender and return the purée to the saucepan. Bring to the boil and add the milk or cream and the lemon juice, and season well with salt and freshly ground black pepper. Heat to blend but do not boil. Cool and chill thoroughly. Garnish each bowl with a sprig of mint and a block of ice. Serve with hot French bread.
Serves 4–6.

Iced Sweet Pepper Soup

400 g red peppers (capsicums)
5 cups tomato juice
2 cloves garlic
salt and white pepper
parsley or other green herbs to garnish

Remove seeds from pepper and blend until smooth with some of the tomato juice and the crushed garlic. Mix this with the remaining tomato juice. Season the soup and chill thoroughly. Blend dry or chopped parsley or other green herbs and use as a garnish for the soup.
Serves 6–8.

La Poule Princesse

Note that this soup is surprisingly rich and only small portions are necessary.

6 cups chicken stock
6 eggs, beaten
4 tablespoons lemon juice
½ teaspoon salt
¼ teaspoon white pepper
3 tablespoons sherry
1 tablespoon curry powder

Bring the chicken stock to slow boil and gradually stir in the beaten eggs to which the lemon juice and seasonings have been added. Add the sherry, remove from the heat and stir in the curry powder. Allow to cool, then chill for several hours. Garnish with a little chopped parsley or chervil.
Serves 6–8.

Senegalese Soup

Superbly refreshing on a hot summer's day.

50 g butter
2 medium onions, coarsely chopped
3 stalks celery, sliced
2 tablespoons flour
1 tablespoon curry powder
2 apples, peeled and chopped
1 cup diced cooked chicken
6 cups chicken stock
1 bay leaf
1 cup cream
desiccated or shredded coconut

Melt the butter in a frying pan. Add the onions and celery and cook until the vegetables are limp but not browned. Add the flour and curry powder and cook, stirring, for several minutes. Purée the apples and chicken with the onion mixture in a blender in three or four batches using enough chicken stock each time to make the purée smooth.

In a saucepan combine the purée mixture with the remainder of the chicken stock, add the bay leaf, bring to the boil, then remove from heat and allow to cool. Remove the bay leaf and chill thoroughly. Add salt if necessary.

Before serving add the cream. Serve garnished with desiccated or shredded coconut which has been toasted to a light golden brown in a frying pan over moderate heat or in a moderate oven.

Serves 10.

Chilled Tomato Soup

250 g onions, peeled and chopped
2 tablespoons oil
500 g tomatoes, quartered
½ teaspoon paprika
3 cups beef stock
whipped cream
chopped parsley

Cook onions in the oil until tender. Stir in tomatoes, cover and simmer gently for 20 minutes. Stir in paprika and beef stock. Purée in a blender and pass through a sieve. Chill. Adjust seasoning after chilling. Serve with a tablespoon of whipped cream swirled into each bowl and garnished with a little chopped parsley.
Serves 6.

Summer Tomato and Yoghurt Soup

A very refreshing soup served very cold with crusty French bread.

2 tablespoons butter
2 medium onions, finely chopped
750 g tomatoes or 3 cups tomato pulp
2 cups water
pepper, salt and sugar to taste
½ teaspoon oregano
1 pot plain yoghurt

Stew the onion in the butter until it is transparent and soft. Add the tomatoes, coarsely chopped, water and seasonings. Simmer gently until the tomatoes and onions are pulp. Put the soup through a sieve, and allow to cool. Stir in the yoghurt, check the seasonings and chill thoroughly.
Serves 6.

Turkish Tomato Soup

A very popular, tangy soup.

3 cups tomato juice
1 cup plain yoghurt
1 tablespoon olive oil
2 tablespoons lemon juice
1½ tablespoons vinegar
½ tablespoon curry powder
2–3 dashes tabasco sauce
1 tablespoon chopped fresh mint or 1 teaspoon dried mint
salt and freshly ground black pepper

Garnish

chopped parsley
chopped fresh basil

Blend all the ingredients, except garnish, in a blender until smooth. Chill. Serve with the garnishes.

Serves 4.

Vichyssoise

In 1910, when the roof garden was opened at the Ritz-Carlton on 46th Street and Madison Avenue, New York, chef Louis Diat celebrated by presenting Manhattan society with a new soup. It was based on a soup his mother had made — the traditional hot leek and potato peasant soup of France. It was refined by the master chef, chilled, and named after the fashionable watering spot Vichy.

4 leeks
3 cups peeled and diced potatoes
2 cups chicken stock
1 tablespoon butter
2 cups milk
1 cup cream
2 teaspoons pepper
paprika
chopped chives

Cut the leeks and about 8 centimetres of their green tops into fine slices, having washed them well first. Cook with the potatoes in about 3 cups boiling water until very tender. Drain, then put through blender or press through a fine strainer and return to saucepan. Add chicken stock, butter, milk, cream, salt and pepper. Mix thoroughly. Reheat — do not boil — to blend. Can be served hot, but much better very cold with a block of ice in each dish. Garnish with paprika and chopped chives.
   Serves 6.

DRIED BEAN, PEA AND LENTIL SOUPS

Some foods are for lovers, some for philosophers, some for tax collectors . . .
When one is near the grave, I prepare for him some lentil soup, and make
the crowning meal of his life glorious.

Athenaeus, circa 200 BC

Dried peas, beans and lentils (or pulses) are all the fruit or edible parts
of plants of the legume family. They are rich, body-building foods and
are very high in vitamins and minerals, especially iron. But note that as these
legumes do not contain vitamin C or A they cannot take the place of fresh
vegetables in the diet. Legumes are a good source of protein for vegetarians
and contain a high fibre content.

They are extremely starchy and must be well cooked to ensure proper
digestion. Usually the legumes are cooked until they are mushy or almost
falling apart. And as a general rule when cooking dried legumes, add the salt
towards the end of cooking as salt hardens protein and makes the vegetables
take longer to cook.

Making soup with dried beans, peas or lentils ensures that all nutriments
and flavour remain, as the water in which the dried vegetables have been

soaked and cooked has absorbed a lot of the food value. Because they contain a high percentage of protein and carbohydrate, the legumes make very healthy and hearty soups. They are excellent too in mixed vegetable and meat soups, as once again they add body and food value. It is best to soak dried legumes — especially peas and beans — overnight or at least for a few hours before cooking, in order to cut down the cooking time. Before soaking it is advisable to wash the dried vegetables as they are often very dusty.

Black Bean and Ham Soup

This soup is especially good if the ham hock or bone has been well smoked.

2 cups dried black beans
10 cups water
ham hock, or ham bone with meat
2 medium onions, chopped
2 carrots, chopped
3 stalks celery, sliced
4 sprigs parsley
3 whole cloves
pinch mace or allspice
pinch thyme
2 bay leaves
1 teaspoon dry mustard
1 tablespoon Worcestershire sauce
½ cup dry sherry
2 eggs, hard-boiled
lemon slices

Soak the beans overnight in plenty of cold water. Drain. In a saucepan combine the beans, water, ham hock, onions, carrots, celery, parsley, cloves, mace, thyme, bay leaves, dry mustard and Worcestershire sauce. Bring to the boil, cover and gently simmer for 2 to 3 hours or until beans are very tender and meat is falling off the ham bone. Remove ham and bone, cutting the meat into very small pieces. Blend the soup or rub it through a sieve. Add the ham and sherry to the purée and season to taste. If soup is too thick (it should be like heavy cream), stir in a little water. Reheat and serve garnished with sliced hard-boiled eggs and lemon slices.

Serves 10–12.

Greek Village Bean Soup

This way of making bean soup is known as Fasolada in Greece and the soup is considered a complete meal in itself.

    1 cup dried beans (white, broad, lima, or yellow or green split peas)
    10 cups cold water
    4 stalks celery, chopped
    2 onions, chopped
    2 carrots chopped
    1 bay leaf
    ¼ cup olive oil
    2 teaspoons salt
    pepper to taste

Wash the beans well, then bring to the boil in the 10 cups water. Reduce the heat and simmer, covered, for 1 hour. Add remaining ingredients, except salt and pepper, and simmer for about 1½ hours or until beans are tender. Add salt the last 10 minutes of cooking time, and add pepper to taste. Serve with water crackers or toast and a cruet of olive oil and vinegar for individual seasoning.

Serves 8.

Italian Bean Soup

Not only delicious but also very substantial, this homely soup is a meal-in-a-bowl especially if served with wads of chunky bread and a green salad.

250 g haricot beans
500 g pork fingers
3 cloves garlic, or more
6 tablespoons fresh chopped parsley, or more
1 large lemon
1 teaspoon dried thyme or 2 teaspoons fresh thyme
1 teaspoon sugar
salt and freshly ground black pepper
1 large onion, finely chopped

Soak the haricot beans overnight in a large bowl of cold water. Lay the pork fingers on the base of a large casserole. Crush the garlic with a little salt and spread it over the pork. Add the chopped parsley, the grated rind of the lemon, the thyme, the sugar and plenty of freshly ground black pepper. Drain, rinse and drain the beans again. Mix them with the chopped onion and pile on top of the pork. Pour on the juice of the lemon, plus 4 cups hot — not boiling — water.

Cover with the lid and cook in the oven very gently, 140°–150°C, gas mark 1–2, for about 4 hours, until the beans are soft and the pork is meltingly tender. Stir in salt to taste, plus extra pepper and/or lemon juice just before serving.

Serves 4.

Kidney Bean Soup

½ cup dried kidney beans
150 g pickled pork
1 medium onion, chopped
1 carrot, diced
3 stalks celery with leaves, sliced
½ bay leaf
3 peppercorns
1 teaspoon ground cumin
salt and freshly ground black pepper to taste
avocado slices
lemon juice

Cover the beans with water and soak them overnight. Drain, discarding the water. Cut the pickled pork into small cubes and cook it slowly in a heavy saucepan to render the fat. Add the onion, carrot and celery to the fat and crisp pork in the saucepan and gently fry them for five minutes. Add the drained beans, 6 cups boiling water, the bay leaf, peppercorns and cumin. Cover and simmer 2½ to 3 hours. Put the soup through a sieve or purée it in a blender. Reheat the soup and correct seasonings with salt and pepper, if needed. Serve the soup topped with avocado slices which have been dipped into the lemon juice.

Serves 6.

Senate Black Bean Soup

Senate or Senator Bean soup was reportedly devised by a cook for the Senators in the Senate Dining Hall in Washington during the Monroe Administration of the early 1800s. Often labelled Mock Turtle soup it has always been a firm favourite in the White House. Here is the original version and the 'translation'.

One pint of black beans soaked overnight in four quarts of water, two onions, one large carrot grated, half pound of fresh beef, half pound of pork, boil all day; when ready for dinner strain through a colander in a tureen; add one wineglass of port wine or not according to fancy, one hard-boiled egg, one lemon slice.

'Translated', the recipe is:
  500 g black beans
  5 litres cold water
  250 g shin beef on bone
  250 g streaky bacon
  2 onions, chopped
  2 carrots, grated
  1 small chilli pepper
  salt and coarsely ground black pepper to taste
  ¾ cup port
  3 hard-boiled eggs, sliced
  12 thin slices lemon

Wash beans, add the water and soak overnight. Add the meat, vegetables and seasonings and simmer 4 to 5 hours. Remove meat and when cool dice the beef and return to the saucepan. Discard the bacon if it has not disintegrated. Purée the soup in a blender or food processor, add the port and reheat. Serve with a slice of egg and a slice of lemon in each cup or soup plate.
  Serves 12.

Chick Pea Soup

The curry flavour improves tremendously if this soup is made a few days in advance and refrigerated until ready to reheat and use.

2 cups chick peas
6 cups water
4 tablespoons olive oil
2 medium onions, finely chopped
1 green pepper, finely chopped
3 cloves garlic, crushed
2 teaspoons curry powder or paste
1 teaspoon ground cumin
salt and pepper
chopped parsley

Wash the chick peas well and soak in the 6 cups cold water overnight. Put the olive oil in a saucepan and lightly fry the onions and green pepper until soft, but not browned. Add the garlic, curry and cumin and the soaked chick peas and the water in which they were soaked. Bring to the boil and simmer for about 30 minutes or until the chick peas are soft. Serve very hot strewn with plenty of chopped parsley.

Serves 6–8.

Chick Pea Soup with Yoghurt

This soup is thick, substantial and wonderful on a cold winter's night with bread and salad.

    250 g chick peas
    3 tablespoons olive oil
    1 large onion, peeled and chopped
    2 cloves garlic, crushed
    1 teaspoon dried oregano
    2 tablespoons tomato paste
    1½ cups chicken stock
    450 g can peeled tomatoes
    tabasco
    salt and pepper
    plain yoghurt

Soak the chick peas in 4 cups water overnight. Cook the peas in the same water by boiling, without salt, for about an hour, or until the peas are soft. Drain the peas and make the liquid up to 4 cups again, with fresh water. In a large saucepan, heat the oil and fry the onion and garlic until soft. Add the oregano, tomato paste, chicken stock and tomatoes. Return the peas and the 4 cups diluted liquor. Simmer for 5 minutes.

Blend half the soup and mash the other half slightly before adding the puréed half. Taste and season well with tabasco and salt and pepper. Reheat and serve piping hot with a spoonful of yoghurt in each bowl.

Serves 4 as a main meal or 8 as a first course.

Dal Soup

Dal or Dhal is the Indian word for lentils. A thick version of this soup is a traditional curry accompaniment.

1 cup red lentils
25 g butter
1 medium onion, finely chopped
1 clove garlic, finely chopped
1 teaspoon finely chopped fresh ginger
½ teaspoon good curry powder
5 cups water
1 teaspoon salt

Wash the lentils. Heat the butter in a saucepan and gently fry the onion, garlic and ginger for a minute. Add the curry powder and continue frying, stirring, for a further few minutes. Add the lentils and water and simmer for about an hour until the lentils are mushy. Stir occasionally whilst cooking. Add the salt. Serve garnished with chopped fresh coriander or parsley.

Serves 4–6.

Brown Lentil Soup

A deliciously robust, peasant-style soup. Nutritious and economical.

500 g brown lentils
2 tomatoes, peeled and coarsely chopped
3 stalks celery, whole
3 cloves garlic, whole
½ cup olive oil
salt to taste

Soak the lentils in a large saucepan overnight. Do not drain, but add enough extra water to cover the soaked lentils well. Add the remaining ingredients, bring to the boil and simmer for about one hour. The lentils should mainly remain whole. Remove the celery and garlic and rub them through a sieve or purée them in a blender. Return purée to the soup. Add salt to taste — it will need plenty — and, if necessary, more water to make a thick consistency. Serve very hot with fried bread croutons or chunks of rye bread. This is more a winter soup but is also excellent served in mugs at an outdoor summer barbecue or in a thermos whilst fishing or boating.

Serves 8–10.

Red Lentil Soup

250 g red lentils
1 large onion, thinly sliced
1 rasher bacon, diced
3 or 4 large tomatoes, peeled and chopped
2 cloves garlic, crushed
1 stick celery, chopped
mint or basil
good dash Worcestershire sauce
250 g frankfurters
bacon fat or oil

Soak the lentils in water overnight. In a large saucepan fry the onion in a generous amount of bacon fat or oil until soft, then add the bacon, tomatoes, garlic and celery. Fry for 5 minutes. Add the strained lentils and stir for a while. Season and add 3 sprigs mint or basil and the Worcestershire sauce. Pour over 2 litres boiling water and cook fairly fast for about an hour or until lentils are soft. Chop the frankfurters in small pieces and add to soup 5 minutes before serving. It does not really need bread or crackers to accompany it. Check seasoning before serving.
Serves 8.

Red Lentil and Veal Soup

500 g red lentils
1 kg veal shank on the bone
1 medium onion, chopped
2 teaspoons salt
black pepper
2 litres boiling water
juice of 2 small lemons
1 teaspoon Worcestershire sauce
chopped parsley
sour cream to garnish

In a casserole or saucepan combine the lentils, veal, onion, salt, pepper and boiling water. Either casserole in moderate oven or simmer on stove for about 1½ hours or until meat is very tender. Remove meat from soup, allow to cool, cut it off the bone into small pieces and return meat to soup. Add lemon juice, Worcestershire sauce and a handful of chopped parsley and cook for a further 10 minutes. Serve garnished with a swirl of sour cream and chopped parsley.
Serves 8–10.

Lima Bean Soup

For vegetarians or people who feel they eat far too much meat, here is an ideal soup.

    2 cups dried lima beans
    8 cups water
    salt
    1 medium onion, chopped
    2 cups sliced celery
    1 medium carrot, cubed
    1 cup cubed potatoes
    2 tablespoons chopped parsley
    juice and grated rind of 1 lemon
    4 tablespoons butter
    dash of cayenne pepper
    3 whole cloves
    dash of pepper

Soak the beans in plenty of water overnight. Drain well, add the 8 cups fresh water and a little salt and gently simmer for an hour. Add the remaining ingredients and continue simmering for a further hour or so, or until the beans are cooked. Add more salt if necessary.

Serves 8.

Navy Bean Soup

A most basic bean soup that is very common in the USA, especially in the south.

    500 g dry navy beans
    10 cups cold water
    1 meaty ham bone
    ½ teaspoon salt
    6 whole black peppercorns
    1 bay leaf
    1 medium onion

Thoroughly wash the beans. Add the cold water, soak overnight (or simmer 2 minutes, then soak 1 hour). Do not drain. Add the ham bone, salt, black peppercorns and bay leaf. Cover and simmer for about 3 to 3½ hours, adding the onion, sliced, the last half hour. Remove ham bone, mash the beans slightly, using a potato masher. Cut the ham off the bone, cube the ham and return it to the soup. Season to taste. Serve with thick slices of brown bread.

Serves 6 generously.

Curried Pea Soup

In this soup it's important you use yellow split peas — simply for the right colour.

    2 cups dried yellow split peas
    6 cups cold water
    2 carrots, chopped
    1 onion, chopped
    1 stalk celery, chopped
    1 clove garlic, chopped
    8 cups chicken stock
    1½ tablespoons curry powder
    1½ cups cream

Soak the peas in water overnight. Drain the peas and combine with the vegetables and stock. Simmer partially covered for an hour. Purée the mixture then add the curry powder, and bring to the boil, then simmer, stirring often, for 20 minutes. Cool, then stir in the cream and add salt and pepper to taste. Serve hot or cold.

Serves 6.

Dutch Pea Soup

Erwtensoep is a main meal dish into which almost anything is flung. It is part of the staple Dutch diet in winter and is usually served in huge bowls with the meat on a side plate. A knife, fork and spoon are provided. You can, however, remove the cooked meat from the soup, cut it into bits and return it — to serve in the soup.

    500 g dried split peas
    3 litres water
    500 g boiling bacon
    1 marrow-bone
    500 g potatoes, peeled and diced
    600 ml milk
    salt and pepper
    2 medium leeks, finely sliced
    2 stalks celery, finely sliced
    chopped parsley

Wash the peas, then soak them overnight in 1.5 litres water. The next day, simmer the bacon and marrow-bone in 1.5 litres boiling water. After an hour, add the peas and the water in which they were soaked and cook until soft — about 1 hour. After about ½ hour of cooking add the potatoes. Take out the marrow-bone and the meat, return the marrow from the bone and the diced bacon to the soup. Coarsely mash the soup and add the milk. Season well and add the leeks and celery and cook for about 20 minutes, stirring occasionally. Before serving, stir in a generous amount of chopped parsley.
Serves 10–12.

Old Fashioned Pea and Ham Soup

    1 bacon knuckle or bacon bones
    500 g green split peas
    2 sprigs mint
    1 large onion, finely chopped
    1 bay leaf

Put all the ingredients in a large saucepan. Fill to three-quarters full with water and bring to the boil. Simmer very slowly for several hours until peas have dissolved. Check seasoning. Cut the meat from the knuckle and cut into small pieces. Return meat to soup and dilute if necessary. Serve piping hot, garnished with sprigs of mint and accompanied by lots of brown bread toast.
Serves 12 or more.

Ol' Quebec Pea Soup

French Canadian Pea soup is very traditional fare especially in the province of Quebec. Here is a typical recipe. Served with crusty bread and cheese and a salad it is excellent.

500 g dried yellow split peas
1 medium onion, finely chopped
3 large carrots, finely chopped
2 stalks celery, finely chopped
1 bay leaf
few sprigs parsley
chicken stock
250 g ham, finely chopped
salt and cracked black pepper

Wash the peas, cover with cold water and soak overnight. In a large saucepan place the peas and the water they were soaked in, plus the onion, carrots, celery, bay leaf and parsley. Cover well with chicken stock, bring to the boil and simmer, covered, for an hour. Add the ham and simmer a further half hour, or until the peas are tender. Season well with salt and cracked pepper. Discard the herbs and purée half the soup in a blender. Return both halves to the saucepan and reheat. Dilute with chicken stock if necessary. Serve piping hot.

Serves 8–10.

Swedish Yellow Pea Soup

For centuries this has traditionally been part of the Thursday supper in Sweden.

2 cups dried yellow split peas
4 cups water
1 pork shank
salt
pinch of ginger and thyme

Rinse the peas and soak them overnight in the water. Bring the peas to the boil in the same water they have been soaked in and add another 4 cups water. Cover and cook rapidly for a few minutes. Add the pork shank. Let the soup simmer for 1 to 1½ hours or until peas have more or less disintegrated and pork is tender. Add more water if the soup becomes too thick. Remove the pork and when cool cut the meat from the bone and chop into pieces and return to the soup. Season the soup with salt, ground ginger and thyme. Serve hot.

Serves 10–12.

Succotash Chowder

1 large onion, chopped
3 tablespoons butter
1 cup whole kernel corn
1 cup cooked lima beans
2 cups cubed potatoes
1 teaspoon salt
pepper
3 cups milk
2 tablespoons flour
parsley

Gently fry the onion in the butter in a saucepan until soft. Add the vegetables, 1 cup water, salt and pepper and simmer, covered, until potato has softened. Add milk and heat to nearly boiling. Blend flour with a little water to make a smooth paste. Stir into soup and cook, stirring, until it has thickened, and the taste of flour has disappeared. Adjust seasonings and serve sprinkled with chopped parsley.

Makes 4 large servings.

HERB SOUPS

No gentleman has soup at luncheon.

Evelyn Waugh

Herbs might be only weeds but they are very elegant weeds that make very elegant soups. A herb soup is usually more suitable as an overture to a dinner than as a meal in itself. This chapter is concerned with the use of herbs in soups, where the herb in each soup provides the dominant flavour. The chapter on Herbs and Spices deals with the use of a herb to enhance the soup, not to make a takeover bid.

The more astringent the herb (sorrel, tarragon, dill, etc.) the more likely it is to make a good soup. Blander herbs can also make excellent soups, however, though their flavour is more subtle. It is a good idea when making a soup using a blander herb to prepare it in advance, in order to allow the particular herb to impart as much flavour as possible to the soup.

We once had a group to dinner who really only liked roast meat and puddings — or thought that was all they liked. Without announcing what it was, we served them a sorrel soup with a few peas in it (so we could call it pea soup, as peas are a very acceptable vegetable). They literally lapped up the soup and declared they had never tasted peas as refreshing as this. They even wanted the recipe. We know that those guests are now herb fanatics because of this soup.

Caraway Seed Soup

For caraway lovers this soup is tremendous — and simple.

50 g butter
8 tablespoons flour
1 tablespoon caraway seeds or ½ tablespoon ground caraway seed
5 cups chicken stock

Melt the butter in a saucepan and stir in the flour. Continually stir over medium heat until the roux becomes light brown. Stir in the caraway seeds and gradually add the stock. Allow to simmer for half an hour, stirring occasionally. Serve with fried croutons.
Serves 4–6.

Chervil Soup

2 large carrots
5 cups chicken or vegetable stock
50 g butter
6 tablespoons flour
4 tablespoons very finely chopped chervil
salt and white pepper to taste

Scrape the carrots and cook in the chicken stock until tender. Remove the carrots and allow to cool so that they can be cut into thick slices. In another saucepan melt the butter, stir in the flour then add half the hot stock. Stir until boiling then simmer, covered for 10 minutes, stirring occasionally, then add remaining stock. Add carrot slices and chervil. Season with salt and white pepper, stir until boiling point and serve.
Serves 6.

Dill Soup

Also good with tarragon or chervil.

2 tablespoons fresh dill, chopped, plus 4 sprigs left whole
25 g butter
2 tablespoons flour
3½ cups good chicken stock
1 egg yolk
1 tablespoon lemon juice
salt and freshly ground black pepper

In a saucepan melt the butter and stir in the flour. Add the hot stock and stir until smooth. Simmer a few minutes. Add the sprigs of dill and salt and pepper and turn off heat. Cover and leave for 30 minutes. Strain the soup then reheat until almost boiling. Beat the egg yolk with the lemon juice in a small bowl. Stir in a cupful of the hot soup. Mix well then pour back into the soup. Stir over low heat for a few minutes. Check the seasonings. Add the chopped dill and serve.
Serves 4.

Creamed Dill Soup

Delicious hot and fantastic cold. If hot, serve with crisp croutons, if cold, garnish with a thin slice of cucumber.

6 cups chicken or vegetable stock
1 medium potato, peeled and cubed
1 medium carrot, grated
1 stalk celery, finely sliced
1 small onion, finely chopped
salt and freshly ground black pepper
2 eggs
½ cup sour cream
6 tablespoons chopped fresh dill or 3 tablespoons dried dill

In a saucepan combine the chicken stock and the prepared vegetables and simmer for about an hour or until the vegetables are very tender. Purée the soup in a blender and return it to the cleaned saucepan. Season the soup well. Mix the 2 eggs, beaten, with the sour cream and the finely chopped dill. Add some of the hot purée to this mixture, slowly, stirring constantly, until you have poured in about 2 cups. Now return it all to the saucepan, and stir well as it heats through. Take care not to let it boil. Note that tarragon can be substituted for the dill.
Serves 6.

Fennel Soup

A warming soup with an unusual flavour.

1 large head Florentine fennel, chopped
25 g butter
1 large onion, chopped
1 clove garlic, crushed
1 large potato, peeled and chopped
4 cups chicken stock
bouquet garni
salt and white pepper
cream
25 g slivered almonds

Slice the fennel and reserve any feathery leaves for garnish. Melt the butter in a saucepan and gently fry the fennel, onion, garlic and potato for 5 minutes. Do not burn. Add the chicken stock, bouquet garni and seasoning and simmer about 30 minutes, until the vegetables are tender. Purée the soup in a blender. Return the purée to the saucepan and reheat. Check the seasoning. Serve with a whirl of cream in each bowl and garnish with slivered almonds and some finely chopped fennel leaves.

Serves 4–6.

French Garlic Soup

You might never suspect what is the basis of this soup. Because the garlic is boiled, the flavour is quite unlike fresh garlic; it is aromatic, delicious and almost indefinable. Around the Mediterranean this soup is considered to be excellent for the liver, blood circulation, general physical tone and spiritual health. Medicine never tasted as good as this.

    16 cloves whole unpeeled garlic
    8 cups water
    2 teaspoons salt
    ½ teaspoon pepper
    2 cloves
    ¼ teaspoon sage
    ¼ teaspoon thyme
    ½ bay leaf
    4 sprigs parsley
    3 tablespoons olive oil
    6 eggs
    6 slices French bread, fried until brown in oil or butter
    chopped parsley
    grated parmesan or romano cheese

Pour boiling water over the garlic and let stand 30 seconds. Drain and peel the garlic. Combine the garlic and all the other ingredients (except the last four) in a large saucepan and simmer for half an hour. Strain the soup into a wide, shallow pan, making sure you push all the garlic through the sieve.

Poach the eggs in the soup. Place a piece of fried bread in each soup bowl, place an egg on top of the bread and ladle soup into the bowl. Garnish each bowl with parsley and pass around the grated cheese.

Serves 6.

Parsley Soup

Very green, very smooth and very good.

    1 small onion
    125 g good parsley
    4 cups chicken stock
    25 g butter
    2 tablespoons flour
    salt and white pepper
    1 medium potato
    1 cup milk

Slice the onion and coarsely chop the parsley. Put the stock in a saucepan and bring to the boil. Add the onion and parsley and simmer, uncovered, for 30 minutes. Purée in a blender. Melt the butter in a saucepan, add the flour, then pour in the purée, season and stir until boiling. Cut the potato into small, even cubes, and simmer in the milk until soft. Then add the potato and milk to the soup. When serving, a swirl of cream can be added to each bowl, if desired.
    Serves 6.

Fresh Spring Herb Soup

Truly refreshing.

    ½ cup chopped herbs (sorrel, parsley, chervil, nettle, tarragon, dandelion, etc.)
    25 g butter or 2 tablespoons oil
    50 g rice
    5 cups chicken stock
    salt
    sour cream

Wash the herbs thoroughly, chop finely and gently fry in the butter or oil for a few minutes. Add the rice (uncooked), stirring all the time, and cook a further few minutes. Stir in the stock gradually and bring to the boil. Cover and simmer for about 10 minutes until rice is tender. Season. Swirl a teaspoon of sour cream into each bowl when serving. As this soup would usually precede a heavy main course, there is no need to serve accompaniments.
    Serves 6.

Highland Nettle Soup

The food value of young nettles has long been known to the Scots, and in *Rob Roy* Sir Walter Scott tells us how it was the practice to force nettles 'for early spring kail' and describes how Andrew Fairservice, the old gardener of Lochleven, raised nettles under hand-glasses for this purpose. The young tops should be gathered when from 9 cm to 20 cm high. They must be very young and pale green otherwise the soup will be bitter. When picking them, gloves should be worn to protect the hands. The nettles should then be washed in running water, using a wooden spoon or a stick, so as not to handle them. Drain and chop finely. Put them in a saucepan with a little water and simmer for about 10 minutes, till tender. Then add about two cups hot milk, season with salt and pepper and thicken with a little cornflour or potato flour worked to a smooth paste with a little butter. Stir well into the soup, bring to the boil and simmer for 10 minutes. Note that the nettles should be cooked for a time otherwise they will be bitter. If you have collected the nettles early enough, they should, without too much imagination being needed, taste somewhat like spinach.

French Sorrel Soup

Very astringent yet very refreshing.

200 g fresh sorrel leaves
50 g butter
3 cups chicken stock
salt and black pepper
2 egg yolks
½ cup cream

Trim the sorrel leaves and wash well. Melt the butter in a saucepan, add the sorrel and cook gently for about 5 minutes. Add the chicken stock, bring to the simmer, cover and simmer for 25 minutes. Put through the blender, mouli or sieve. Return to the saucepan and reheat. Add salt and black pepper to taste. Beat the egg yolks with the cream, stir in a ladleful of the hot soup, then return the mixture to the saucepan. Heat thoroughly without boiling and serve at once.
Serves 4.

Sorrel and Lettuce Soup

This is smashing, either hot or chilled, with or without the cream and with a selection of fresh herbs added at the same time as the sorrel and lettuce.

 50 g butter
 1 large onion, finely chopped
 1 medium lettuce, washed and chopped
 1 bunch sorrel, washed and chopped
 5 cups chicken stock
 1 cup cream
 salt and pepper

Heat the butter in a saucepan, add onion and fry until soft over a low heat. Add the lettuce and sorrel and cook in the butter for a few minutes then add the stock. Bring to the boil, cover and simmer 5–7 minutes. Purée in a blender. Return purée to the saucepan, bring to the boil and remove from the heat. Gradually add the cream, stirring all the time, and season well with salt and white pepper. Serve with cheese straws.

Serves 6.

Tarragon Soup

Nothing could be simpler than this soup, yet it is so good and so suitable before a large meal. Fresh tarragon is imperative.

To 6 cups of good (home-made) chicken, meat or fish stock add 4 teaspoons finely chopped fresh tarragon. Heat slowly in a saucepan and just before serving stir in 2 tablespoons grated parmesan cheese. If you prefer, a richer soup can be attained by the addition of cream or eggs. However, this soup's charm is its lightness.

Serves 6.

CHEESE SOUPS

Rats! They fought the dogs and killed the cats,
And bit the babies in the cradles,
And ate the cheeses out of the vats
And licked the soup from the cooks' own ladles.
Robert Browning, *The Pied Piper of Hamelin*

Today there are several thousand types of cheese in the world, and of these France claims over 500 varieties. Despite this wide field, however, no attempt has ever been made to create a really great cheese soup. Considering cheeses have been around since at least 4000 BC, it is surprising that no cuisine has ever developed a classic soup using cheese. Switzerland does have a bread and cheese soup though it is more a variation on the fondue than a soup. Perhaps the only classic is Rinctum Diddy which is an American soupy version of the Welsh Rabbit by way of the tomato-flavoured Russian Rabbit or Rarebit. However, some of the main types of cheese make very admirable soups, either by themselves or in combination with a compatible vegetable.

Blue Cheese Soup

Served hot and fresh with wholewheat bread, this soup is quite an experience.

2 tablespoons butter
2 tablespoons flour
5 cups chicken stock
white pepper
3 tablespoons parsley, chopped
½ cup cream
4 tablespoons blue vein cheese, grated or crumbled
salt to taste

Melt the butter in a saucepan and stir in the flour. Gradually add the chicken stock and slowly bring to the boil, stirring often. Allow to simmer for a few minutes, then season with white pepper. Just before serving, add the chopped parsley, cream and cheese. Add salt if necessary, heat through and serve at once.
Serves 6.

Broccoli and Cheese Soup

Absolutely scrumptious. Use more broccoli if you like for a really thick green soup.

25 g butter
1 medium onion, finely chopped
500 g broccoli
5 cups chicken stock
salt and freshly ground black pepper
1 teaspoon sugar
¾ cup cream
60 g grated gruyere cheese

Melt the butter in a saucepan and gently fry the onion until soft, but not browned. Peel any hard stem from the broccoli and discard most outer leaves, if any. Coarsely chop the stalks and heads. Add the broccoli to the saucepan and pour in the chicken stock. Bring to the boil, cover and simmer gently for 20 minutes, or until the broccoli is tender. Purée the soup in a blender and return it to the rinsed saucepan. Reheat, check the seasoning and add the sugar. Add the cream and grated cheese, heat thoroughly and serve with a little extra cream swirled into each bowl.
Serves 6.

Celery and Cheese Soup

8 large stalks celery
2 tablespoons butter
grated nutmeg
2 cups chicken stock
1 tablespoon pea flour
1 cup milk
salt and freshly ground black pepper
grated medium cheddar cheese

Finely slice the celery stalks and finely chop some of the leaves. Put these in a saucepan with the butter and a little freshly grated nutmeg and gently fry for about 5 minutes without browning the celery. Add the chicken stock, cover, and simmer until the celery is barely tender, about half an hour.

Mix the pea flour, or cornflour, with a little of the milk and stir into the soup and simmer for a further few minutes. Stir in the remaining milk and season to taste with salt and freshly ground black pepper. Do not oversalt the soup. Reheat to blend. Serve liberally covered with grated cheese.

Serves 4.

Cheddar Cheese Soup

Nourishing, heartening and warming.

¼ cup finely sliced spring onion
50 g butter
3 tablespoons flour
3 cups chicken stock
¾ cup diced celery
¾ cup diced carrot
salt and white pepper
2 cups grated tasty cheddar cheese
1 cup milk
dash of cayenne pepper
4 rashers bacon
chopped parsley

In a saucepan gently fry the spring onions in the butter for a few minutes, then stir in the flour to make a smooth roux. Remove saucepan from heat and slowly add the chicken stock, stirring. Return pan to heat and cook, stirring, until smooth and thickened. Add the celery and carrot, and salt and pepper to taste, and cook over moderate heat for about 20 minutes or until the vegetables are tender. Stir in the cheese and the milk and add the cayenne. Cook, stirring, until the cheese has melted. Simmer the soup for 5 minutes and check the seasoning.

Dice the bacon and fry in a frying pan until crisp. Drain it well and serve the soup garnished with some bacon and chopped parsley. Serve with crusty bread.

Serves 4.

Cheese and Lager Soup

2 tablespoons butter
½ cup grated carrot
¼ cup grated onion
¼ cup flour
salt and black pepper
2 teaspoons chicken stock powder
2½ cups milk
2 cups grated erbo cheese (an Italian cheese similar to gorgonzola)
½ cup lager
1 tablespoon chopped parsley

In a saucepan melt the butter, add the carrot and onion and cook gently until tender, but not browned. Blend in the flour and seasonings. Add the milk all at once and stir over low heat until thickened. Add cheese and stir until it melts. Just before serving blend in lager and parsley and heat through.

Serves 4.

Cottage Cheese Soup

Warming and nourishing and deliciously creamy.

1 tablespoon butter
1 cup thinly sliced celery
½ cup chopped spring onion
2 tablespoons flour
3 cups milk
3 teaspoons chicken stock powder
½ teaspoon paprika
white pepper
grated nutmeg
salt
1 clove garlic, crushed
1 cup cottage cheese

Melt the butter in a saucepan, add the celery and onion, and cook over medium heat for about 5 minutes or until vegetables are crisp-tender. Stir in the flour, add milk and chicken stock powder or cubes. Cook and stir until mixture comes to the boil. Stir in paprika, pepper, nutmeg and salt to taste, the crushed garlic and the cheese. Heat just to boiling point and serve at once.

Serves 4.

Rinctum Diddy

A thick-soup version of Russian Rarebit, excellent for lunch or a light evening meal served with thin toast or on egg noodles.

3 tablespoons butter
1 small onion, finely chopped
1 tablespoon flour
2 tablespoons dry red wine
3 cups tomato soup
½ teaspoon dry mustard
½ teaspoon salt
¼ teaspoon pepper
pinch ground cloves
350 g tasty cheddar cheese, cut into small pieces
¼ teaspoon baking soda
1 egg, lightly beaten

Cook the onion in the butter until soft and yellow, add the flour and when it is well blended, add the wine and tomato soup. Stir in the seasonings, then add the cheese, stirring until the cheese is melted. Add the soda, then the lightly beaten egg. Stir until smooth. Serve with hot, thin toast or egg noodles, accompanied, if you wish, by more dry red wine.

Serves 6.

FRUIT SOUPS

An idealist is one who, on noticing that a rose smells better than a cabbage,
concludes that it will also make better soup.

H.L. Mencken, *Chrestomathy 617*

Fruit soups originated in Scandinavia where they are usually served as a dessert.
However, in Germany they constitute a chilled summer appetiser before the
main meal, a trend that has appeared in many other countries. After all, if we can
serve fruit as an appetiser or as part of the first course or main course why not
accept fruit in the soup? Fruit soups are usually astringent and refreshing and
lightly spiced. They make ideal chilled soups though some can be served hot also.

The good thing about fruit soups too is that you can use partially spoiled
fruit, such as peaches or plums, that otherwise would be stewed or wasted. And
of course, when the fruits are in season the soup can be comparatively cheap
to make. Since these soups are usually very light and often spicy, they make an
ideal starter to any summer meal — or a winter meal for that matter.

Some of your favourite fruits may be missing from this chapter. Select a
recipe using a similar fruit and invent your own masterpiece. For instance,
you could try substituting guavas, feijoas or passionfruit for kiwifruit in the
Chilled Kiwifruit soup. Or use boysenberries, blackcurrants or blueberries in
the Blackberry soup, or maybe substitute persimmons for apricots.

Iced Apple Soup

Adults and children alike love this soup. Try serving it for breakfast too. It is excellent for wakening palates.

3 cloves
1 cinnamon stick
½ cup water
2 tablespoons sugar
1 teaspoon lemon juice
2 cups apple sauce
1 cup cream
lemon slices

In a saucepan combine the cloves, cinnamon stick and water. Bring to the boil, then allow to cool. Remove spices and add the sugar, lemon juice and apple sauce. Lightly whip the cream and fold into the apple mixture. Chill thoroughly before serving. Serve garnished with a little whipped cream and a lemon slice.
Serves 4.

Apple Vichyssoise

This makes a refreshing change from the classic Vichyssoise — different but still scrumptious.

2 large potatoes, chopped
2 stalks celery, sliced
2 eating apples, peeled and chopped
1 large onion, peeled and chopped
3 cups chicken stock
1 teaspoon curry powder
1 tablespoon butter
salt and white pepper
1 cup cream
snipped chives

In a saucepan combine the potatoes, celery, apples, onion and chicken stock. Bring to the boil and simmer, covered, for about 15 minutes or until vegetables are tender. Purée the mixture in a blender or rub it through a sieve. Return the purée to the saucepan and add the curry powder, butter, salt and pepper to taste. Simmer for 5 minutes. Remove from heat, stir in cream and chill thoroughly. Serve garnished with snipped chives.

Serves 6.

Apricot and Carrot Soup

An usual flavour that is quite stunning for a dinner party.

½ cup dried apricots
250 g carrots
2 medium onions
1 medium potato
3 tablespoons butter
5 cups chicken stock
2 bay leaves
salt and white pepper
2 tablespoons cream
2 egg yolks
3 rashers lean bacon
1 tablespoon sherry

Peel and chop carrots, onions and potato. Heat the butter in a saucepan and add vegetables. Cook slowly over low heat for about 5 minutes. Add apricots, chicken stock, bay leaves, season and bring to the boil. Simmer 1 hour until soft. Remove bay leaves and purée soup. Beat cream and egg yolks together and slowly beat into soup. Add sherry and check seasoning. Fry or grill the bacon until very crisp. Drain, allow to cool, then break it into bits. Serve the soup garnished with the bacon bits.

Serves 6–8.

Blackberry Soup

Any similar berry can be used for this unusual soup.

2½ cups blackberries
2 small lemons, sliced
2 cups water
2½ cm stick cinnamon
2 cloves
½ cup sugar
2 cups sour cream

In a saucepan combine the first six ingredients. Bring to the boil and simmer for 10 minutes. Rub the soup through a sieve. Allow to cool, add the sour cream, then chill thoroughly.

Serves 6.

Caribbean Banana Soup

A fairly hearty soup, although when accentuated by coconut it is not notably sweet. And it is good cold, too.

6 bananas
4 cups beef stock
½ cup finely chopped onion
¼ cup diced green pepper
2 cloves garlic, finely chopped
2 tablespoons oil
1 cup freshly grated coconut
hot pepper sauce
pepper and salt
toasted coconut

In a large saucepan mash the bananas coarsely, add the beef stock and simmer, stirring occasionally, for 10 minutes. In a frying pan gently fry the onion, green pepper and garlic, in the oil, until the vegetables are softened. Add the freshly grated coconut — or dried shredded coconut — and cook a few minutes more. Add the coconut mixture to the banana mixture and season well with hot pepper sauce, pepper and salt. Simmer for 30 minutes. Serve garnished with toasted coconut.

Serves 6–8.

Chilled Kiwifruit Soup

Kiwifruit is an insidious new title for Chinese Gooseberries or their correct Chinese title *Yang Tao*. However, this soup is delightfully refreshing and quite a thin soup. If you prefer it thicker, cornflour or arrowroot can be used to thicken the syrup.

3 whole cloves
1 small piece cinnamon stick
sprig of mint
1 cup water
4 tablespoons sugar
500 g very ripe kiwifruit
1 cup cream
1 teaspoon lemon juice
chopped mint and kiwifruit slices to garnish

In a saucepan combine the cloves, cinnamon, mint, water and sugar. Bring to boil, allow to cool, then remove the spices and mint. Peel the kiwifruit, reserving one for the garnish, and mash them, then rub them through a sieve to remove the seeds (which tend to be bitter). Add the purée to the syrup and add the cream and lemon juice. Stir well and refrigerate until thoroughly chilled. Serve in chilled bowls garnished with a slice of kiwifruit and a little chopped mint.
Serves 4.

Kiwifruit and Wine Soup

2½ cups peeled and diced kiwifruit
2 cups Sauternes or other sweet white wine
1 cup water
¼ cup sugar
dash salt
1 tablespoon cornflour
whipped cream to garnish

In a saucepan combine the kiwifruit, 1 cup of wine, water, sugar and salt. Bring to the boil and cook over medium heat for 5 minutes. Dissolve the cornflour in ¼ cup remaining wine and stir mixture into soup and boil 1 minute, stirring constantly. Remove from heat and stir in remaining wine. Put half of soup into blender container. Cover and blend until puréed. Stir purée into remaining soup. Chill well. Serve garnished with whipped cream.
Serves 4–6.

Spiced Cherry Soup

Delightfully excellent before a gargantuan meal, for instance Christmas dinner.

500 g cherries
3 whole cloves
1 small stick cinnamon
1 cup sugar
5 cups water
3 tablespoons cornflour
1 cup red wine
½ teaspoon grated lemon rind
lemon juice to taste
sour cream to garnish

Cook the berries, cloves, cinnamon, sugar and water until the cherries are tender. Remove the spices. Dissolve the cornflour in the wine, add the lemon rind and lemon juice and stir it into the cherry liquid. Cook until clear. Serve chilled with a topping of sour cream.
Serves 6.

Hot Curried Grapefruit Soup

If you find grapefruit or gold fruit too bitter use oranges instead.

25 g butter
½ cup brown sugar
2 teaspoons curry powder
dash tabasco sauce
2 cups water
1 cup grapefruit juice
2 grapefruit

In a saucepan melt the butter and add the sugar, curry powder, tabasco, water and grapefruit juice. Bring to the boil and simmer a few minutes. Peel the grapefruit, remove as much of the white membrane as possible and cut it into pieces. Just before serving add the grapefruit, heat through and serve piping hot.
Serves 4.

Cream of Lemon Soup

Surprisingly refreshing, yet surprisingly rich.

25 g butter
100 g onions, peeled and sliced
100 g carrots, peeled and sliced
4 cups chicken stock
1 large lemon
bouquet garni
1 tablespoon arrowroot
salt and freshly ground black pepper
¾ cup cream

Melt the butter in a large saucepan and cook the prepared vegetables until tender, stirring frequently to prevent browning. Add the stock, bring to the boil, then reduce the heat and simmer. Using a potato peeler, thinly peel the rind from the lemon. Pour boiling water over the rind, leave for one minute, then drain. Add the rind and juice of the lemon and the bouquet garni to the saucepan. Cover and cook for 1 hour or until the vegetables are really soft. Remove the bouquet garni, leave the lemon rind, and purée the soup, a little at a time, in the blender. In a clean saucepan, blend the arrowroot with a little of the soup, then add the remainder, stirring. Bring to the boil, stirring. Adjust the seasoning before adding the cream. Reheat but do not boil. As a garnish, swirl a little extra cream into each bowl. Serve by itself.

Serves 4–6.

Cold Orange and Pear Soup

The fruit for this soup should be very ripe.

    2 oranges
    2 large pears
    2½ cups orange juice
    2½ cups water
    8 tablespoons honey
    grated rind and juice of 1 lemon or lime
    2 tablespoons cornflour
    1 tablespoon cold water

Peel the oranges, peel and core the pears and cut the fruit into small pieces. Combine with the orange juice and water in a saucepan, bring to the boil and simmer until the fruit is soft. Add the honey, grated lemon rind and lemon juice. Mix the cornflour to a paste with the cold water, and add to the soup. Bring to the boil, stirring, and simmer for 5 minutes. Allow to cool, then refrigerate until very cold.

Serves 6.

Peach Soup

    500 g ripe peaches
    3 cups water
    ½ cup sugar
    pinch ground cloves
    ¼ teaspoon ground allspice
    1 cup dry white wine
    3 tablespoons semolina

In a saucepan, combine the peaches, water, sugar, cloves and allspice. Bring to the boil and simmer for 20 minutes. Blend to a purée then return to saucepan. Add the wine, bring to the boil and thicken with the semolina mixed with a little water. Allow to cool, then chill thoroughly. Serve garnished with a blob of whipped cream and maybe a slice of fresh peach.

Serves 6.

Chilled Plum Soup

500 g plums
1 litre water
2 strips lemon peel
1 cinnamon stick
6 tablespoons sugar
1 cup dry red wine
3 tablespoons cornflour or semolina
3 tablespoons cold water

Halve the plums and remove the stones. Place in saucepan with water, lemon peel and cinnamon stick. Slowly bring to the boil, cover and simmer until fruit is tender. Remove lemon peel and cinnamon. Add sugar and cook until dissolved. In a blender, blend fruit and wine together, returning purée to saucepan. If desired, the soup need not be blended at all. Mix cornflour with the 3 tablespoons water and stir into soup. Cook, stirring, until soup comes to the boil and thickens. Allow to cool and chill.

Serves 6–8.

Cold Raspberry Soup

A most refreshing summer soup. Some love it, some hate it, but no one has ever been indifferent about it.

500 g fresh or frozen raspberries
2 tablespoons honey
5 tablespoons red wine
1 small carton sour cream

Rub the raspberries through a fine sieve. This should give about 300 ml purée. Put the honey, together with 2 tablespoons wine, in a small saucepan and heat gently until the honey is dissolved. Leave for a few minutes to cool and then stir into the raspberry purée. Stir in half the sour cream. Add the rest of the wine and 200 ml cold water. Stir again and chill for several hours. Serve in bowls with spoonfuls of sour cream floating on top. Serve with extra sour cream.

Serves 4.

Strawberry Soup

Most refreshing and most agreeable, especially before a spicy or heavy main course.

juice of 1 lemon
1 teaspoon finely grated lemon rind
2 cups water
1 cup sugar
2 tablespoons arrowroot
1 cup orange juice
1 cup sweet white wine
2 chips very ripe strawberries, mashed

In a saucepan, combine lemon juice, lemon rind, water and sugar and bring to the boil. Make a paste with arrowroot and a little cold water, and stir into the soup. Stir until thickened and cover and simmer for 10 minutes. Add well-mashed strawberries, orange juice and white wine and stir to mix. Bring to boil and serve piping hot, or cool and chill and serve very cold. Serve with fancy crackers, if you wish.
Serves 6–8.

Scandinavian Fruit Soup

250 g dried apricots or 500 g fresh apricots
4 cooking apples, peeled, cored and sliced
1½ cups strong beef stock
1 bay leaf
few sprigs parsley
2 stalks celery, left whole
1 teaspoon salt
pepper
4 cups milk
cream

If using dried apricots soak them in 2½ cups boiling water overnight. If using fresh apricots, wash and remove stones. In a saucepan combine apricots, apples, beef stock and herbs, celery and seasoning. Bring to the boil and simmer, covered, gently, for 20–30 minutes or until fruit is soft. Remove celery, parsley and bay leaf. Either blend soup to a purée or rub it through a sieve. Allow to cool. Season carefully, then stir in the milk. Dilute with more milk if necessary. Chill. Serve garnished with cream whipped with a little salt.
Serves 6.

Tamarillo Soup

Tamarillos (or, as they were once called, tree tomatoes) make a surprisingly refreshing chilled soup.

    500 g very ripe tamarillos
    6 whole allspice
    small piece cinnamon stick
    ¼ teaspoon grated nutmeg
    1 tablespoon cornflour
    ¼ cup brown sugar
    1½ cups water
    1 cup cream
    whipped cream to garnish

Either peel the tamarillos or cut them in half and scoop the flesh out with a spoon. Chop up the flesh and in a saucepan combine it with the spices, cornflour, sugar and water. Bring to the boil and simmer until the fruit is tender, about 5 minutes. Allow to cool. Sieve the soup, pushing through as much of the tamarillos as possible. Refrigerate until ready to serve. Before serving add the cup of cream. Serve with a swirl of whipped cream in each bowl.
Serves 4.

Watermelon Soup

    1 medium watermelon
    1½ cups dry white wine
    ¾ cup water
    ½ cup honey
    4 slices lemon or lime
    1 vanilla bean
    fresh mint

Cut melon and make about a dozen balls from the seedless portion. Place in bowl with wine and chill. Heat water in saucepan and add honey, lemon slices and vanilla bean, and simmer, covered, for 20 minutes. Allow to cool. Remove citrus and vanilla. Seed and cube 3 cups melon, place in blender along with the honey water and blend until smooth. Combine mixture with the melon ball mixture and chill thoroughly. Serve garnished with chopped fresh mint.
Serves 6.

NUT AND SEED SOUPS

I believe I once considerably scandalized her by declaring that clear soup
was a more important factor in life than a clear conscience.
'Saki' (H.H. Munro), *The Blind Spot*

Nut soups are fairly rare, probably because there are not many varieties of
nuts and also because when whole nuts are boiled they tend to lose flavour
and palatability. However, when nuts are grown in abundance, a nut soup is usually
included in the nation's cuisine, such as East Africa's Peanut (Groundnut) soup
or Mexico's Almond soup. With today's emphasis on healthy foods, cereals and
seeds are in vogue. The most popular of these, brown rice, barley and sunflower
seeds are all included here — not a lengthy list, but an introduction to a kind of
soup that has unlimited possibilities. After all, dried peas and beans — standard
soups in many countries — are seeds too. Note that as the peanut is regarded
more often as a nut than a legume it has been included in this chapter rather
than the Dried Bean chapter. It is generally accepted that nuts, although a rich
food, are regarded as rather indigestible unless thoroughly chewed. Cashew nuts
for instance become rather difficult to digest when boiled. Fortunately most nuts
become very acceptable when finely chopped or puréed in soups.

Mexican Almond Soup

Delightfully nutty and pleasantly refreshing.

2 tablespoons butter
2 tablespoons flour
3 cups beef stock
pinch each of nutmeg, thyme and mace
1 whole clove
1 cup ground almonds
1 cup cream
1½ cups milk
salt and white pepper to taste
¼ cup toasted slivered almonds

Melt the butter in a saucepan and blend in the flour. Remove from heat and gradually add stock, stirring constantly. Return to heat and bring to the boil, still stirring. Add nutmeg, thyme, mace, clove and ground almonds. Reduce heat and simmer for 30 minutes. Strain the soup through a sieve into a clean saucepan, rubbing as much of the almond through as possible. Add cream and milk and heat to serving temperature. Season with salt and pepper and serve garnished with toasted slivered almonds.

Serves 6.

Almond Soup with Meatballs

An unusual soup that is quite stunning.

3 tablespoons oil
½ cup blanched almonds
1 slice bread, cubed
1 clove garlic, sliced
2 tablespoons finely chopped onion
2 tablespoons butter
2 tablespoons flour
6 cups chicken stock
500 g minced pork or veal
2 slices bread soaked in milk
1 egg
1 teaspoon salt
freshly ground black pepper
¼ cup tomato sauce

In the oil, gently fry the almonds, bread, and garlic until golden and crisp. When cool enough, finely chop them. In a large saucepan fry the onion in the butter until onion is golden then stir in the flour. Gradually add the chicken stock and bring to the boil, stirring continuously. Form the minced pork, crumbled soaked bread, egg, salt and pepper into balls and drop into the boiling stock and simmer for 25 minutes. Add the almond mixture and the tomato sauce and check the seasonings. Simmer a further 5 minutes and serve piping hot.

Serves 8.

Barley, Bean and Mushroom Soup

A fairly substantial soup for vegetarians and barley lovers especially.

1 large onion, finely chopped
1 clove garlic, crushed
2 tablespoons butter or oil
250 g mushrooms, sliced
6 cups vegetable stock
½ cup dried baby lima beans, soaked overnight
1 cup pearl barley, washed
1 bunch parsley, finely chopped
pinch each of nutmeg, thyme and ginger
1 clove
salt and cracked black pepper

In a large saucepan gently fry the onion and garlic in the butter or oil until soft but not browned. Add the mushrooms, lower the heat, and cook covered for 10 minutes. Add the stock and remaining ingredients, cover and simmer for 1½ hours, stirring occasionally. Serve hot with rye bread. If a thinner soup is desired, dilute with more stock.

Serves 6–8.

Chestnut Soup

½ cup finely chopped carrot
½ cup finely chopped celery
½ cup finely chopped onion
3 tablespoons butter
8 cups chicken stock
bouquet garni
2 cups crumbled cooked chestnuts
¼ cup madeira
¼ cup cream
salt and pepper

In a large saucepan gently fry the carrot, celery and onion in the butter until tender, about 15 minutes, taking care not to burn them. Add the chicken stock and the bouquet garni and simmer for 20 minutes. Add the cooked chestnuts and madeira and simmer for 3 minutes. Remove the bouquet garni and purée the soup in a blender or food processor. Return the purée to the cleaned saucepan and add the cream and season with salt and white pepper. Heat until hot but do not boil.

Note that cooked Brussels sprouts can be added to the soup before it is puréed to make another delicious soup. And note that to shell and cook chestnuts, cut off the tops and bake them in a moderate oven or grill them for 20 minutes.

Serves 6–8.

Carrot Soup with Rolled Oats

Smooth, delicious and . . . terribly, terribly healthy.

    1 kg carrots, scraped and sliced
    2 stalks celery, chopped
    2 onions, peeled and chopped
    50 g butter
    2 teaspoons sugar
    2 teaspoons salt
    10 cups vegetable or light chicken stock
    sprig of thyme
    ¾ cup rolled oats
    chopped parsley

Melt the butter in a large saucepan. Add the carrots, celery, onions, sugar and salt and sweat them for a few minutes, stirring. Pour on warm stock and add sprig of thyme. Bring to a quiet simmer, cover and cook for 2 hours. Remove the thyme and purée everything in a blender, mouli or sieve and return to the saucepan. Sprinkle in the rolled oats and season with salt. Simmer, stirring occasionally, for 10 minutes. Garnish with parsley.

Serves 8.

Fijian Coconut Soup

Smooth and refreshing and an ideal hot weather soup.

    1 tablespoon butter
    2 tablespoons flour
    ½ teaspoon curry powder
    salt and white pepper
    2½ cups milk
    1 tablespoon tomato sauce
    2 cups coconut cream
    toasted coconut to garnish

In a saucepan melt the butter and stir in the flour, curry powder, salt and pepper. Cook for a few minutes then gradually add the milk. Add the tomato sauce. Stir constantly over low heat until boiling. Simmer for a few minutes. Just before serving add the coconut cream, check the seasoning, heat through and serve garnished with toasted coconut.

Serves 6–8.

Brown Rice Soup

So good yet so simple to make. It is a bit like a very elegant barley soup.

4 tablespoons brown rice
1 tablespoon oil
1 small onion, finely chopped
1 leek, finely chopped
some celery or celeriac, finely chopped
1 small carrot, finely sliced
5 cups chicken or vegetable stock
2 teaspoons parsley, chopped fresh
2 teaspoons chervil, chopped fresh
1 teaspoon basil, chopped fresh
a little butter

Rinse and drain the rice. Gently fry the onion in the oil. Add the remaining vegetables and gently fry for a few minutes. Add boiling stock and allow to cook until rice is tender, about half an hour. Add all the herbs and leave to stand in a warm place for 15 minutes. Before serving add a nut of butter.

Serves 4–6.

Cream of Barley Soup

½ cup peal barley
5 cups well-seasoned chicken stock
25 g butter
1 tablespoon flour
salt and pepper
½ cup milk
¼ cup cream
1 carrot
1 small turnip
3 tablespoons green peas

Wash the barley and soak it overnight in 1½ cups water. Add the barley and water to the stock and simmer for about an hour or until barley is tender. Strain, reserving several tablespoons of cooked barley for a garnish. Rinse the saucepan and in it make a roux with the butter and flour, and cook it for a few minutes. Season. Pour on the stock, stirring, bring to the boil and simmer for 5 minutes. Add the milk and cream and the reserved barley. Continue to simmer while preparing the vegetables. Cut the carrot and turnip into small dice and steam them, along with the green peas until tender. Add to the soup and serve.
Serves 6.

Brazil Nut Soup

Hazel nuts can also be used for this pleasantly rich soup.

100 g brazil nuts, finely chopped
4 cups good chicken stock
1 small onion, sliced
1 small leek, sliced
1 small stalk celery, sliced
50 g butter
1 tablespoon flour
salt and pepper
½ cup cream
pinch of mace

Put the chopped nuts in a heavy saucepan with the chicken stock. Bring to the boil and simmer for 10 minutes. Slice the onion, leek and celery. Melt the butter in a frying pan and gently fry the vegetables for 5 minutes. Add them to the stock. Mix the flour to a smooth paste with cold water and stir into the soup. Bring to the boil, stirring, and simmer covered for about 25 minutes. Season to taste with salt and freshly ground black pepper and just before serving stir in the cream and mace.

Serves 4–6.

Karanga Peanut Soup

An East African soup that is equally nice hot and cold.

    250 g peanuts (skinned and ground to a powder)
    1 onion
    1 stalk celery
    2½ cups milk
    25 g butter
    4 tablespoons flour
    3 cups chicken stock
    4 tablespoons cream
    salt and white pepper
    chopped parsley

Put nuts (best ground in an electric coffee grinder) in saucepan with finely chopped onion, celery and milk. Simmer 1 hour, then rub through a sieve. Melt the butter in the flour and cook slightly, then add the stock and bring to the boil, stirring all the time. Add the nuts and milk mixture. Heat to boiling. Just before serving add the cream and seasoning to taste. Season it well. Serve garnished with the chopped parsley.

Serves 6.

Peanut and Tomato Soup

African inspired, this sounds a rather strange combination but it is really quite marvellous.

2 tablespoons peanut oil
2 teaspoons ground cumin
2 teaspoons coriander
pinch chilli powder
½ cup smooth peanut butter
6 cups beef stock
500 g peeled and chopped tomatoes
1 green pepper, finely chopped
chopped parsley to garnish

In a saucepan, heat the oil, add the spices and peanut butter and gently fry for several minutes. Slowly stir in the stock, add the tomatoes and simmer for 10 minutes. Add the chopped green pepper, season with salt if necessary and simmer a further few minutes. Serve very hot, garnished with chopped parsley, or if you have it, fresh coriander.

Serves 6–8.

Virginia Peanut Soup

Excellent served before a very spicy main course.

100 g butter
100 g peanut butter
2 tablespoons flour
5 cups chicken stock
½ cup hot cream
1 tablespoon butter (extra)

Melt the butter, add the peanut butter and stir for 3 minutes. Add the flour and stir until golden brown, then add the Chicken stock and salt to taste. Simmer gently for 25 minutes. Strain and reheat the soup. Just before serving add the hot cream and the extra butter. Stir and serve hot with plain wheaten biscuits.

Serves 4–6.

Hazel Nut and Asparagus Soup

It sounds an unusual combination but it really is quite delicious and is well worth making despite the laborious peeling of the hazel nuts.

½ cup hazel nuts
1 tablespoon butter
1 medium onion, chopped
100 g cooked ham
5 cups chicken stock
¼ cup dry sherry
salt and freshly ground black pepper
½ cup cream
350 g canned or fresh asparagus

Cover the hazel nuts with boiling water and let stand for at least 6 minutes. Drain and remove skins. Repeat the blanching if the skins are still unwilling to leave the nuts. Dry the hazel nuts thoroughly and gently fry them in the butter until golden but not burnt. Remove from the butter and set aside. Gently fry the onion in the remaining butter until limp but not brown. Combine the nuts, onion, ham and some of the stock in a blender and blend to a smooth paste. Heat the remaining stock; add the sherry and nut mixture, stirring to blend well. Taste for seasoning, and simmer about 15 minutes. Remove from heat and add the cream and asparagus cut into bite-sized pieces. Reheat the soup without allowing it to come to the boil. Note that instead of asparagus, cooked your broad beans or shredded spinach can be substituted.

Serves 6.

Sunflower Seed Soup

Sweetish and nutty, this soup is quite unusual, yet very popular.

½ chicken
2 tablespoons honey
1 green pepper, chopped
2 large tomatoes, peeled and chopped
1 medium onion, chopped
1 cup sunflower seed kernels
1 cup peas
salt and pepper

Put the half chicken in a saucepan, cover with water, add the honey and some salt and pepper. Bring to the boil and simmer until the chicken is tender. When cool enough to handle, remove the chicken from the stock and remove the flesh from the bones. Chop the flesh coarsely and return it to the stock. Add the green pepper, tomatoes, onion and sunflower seed kernels, bring to the boil and simmer until the vegetables are tender. Purée the soup in a blender and return it to the saucepan. Add the peas, and check the seasoning. Reheat before serving. The soup should be fairly thick but if it is too thick add some more chicken stock.

Serves 6–8.

Rourou

A Fijian soup that is very popular and very easy to prepare. Theoretically it should be made from dalo (taro) leaves, but silver beet or spinach can effectively be substituted.

    400 g young taro leaves, or silver beet or spinach
    2 cups coconut cream
    1 teaspoon salt

Wash the greens well, coarsely chop them and put in a saucepan along with the coconut cream and salt. Bring to the boil, cover and simmer for 15 minutes. Purée the soup in a blender or food processor, check the seasoning and reheat before serving.
Serves 4.

To make Coconut Cream
Besides using the flesh of fresh coconuts or using a can of coconut cream, you can easily make the cream from desiccated coconut and milk. To make 2 cups coconut cream, bring to the boil 2 cups milk and 2 cups desiccated coconut. Remove from heat, and when cool enough to handle, strain the cream through muslin. Discard the desiccated coconut.

Variations
Dilute the soup with chicken stock (or better still, fish stock). And if you wish add a squeeze or two of lemon or lime juice.

Walnut Soup

Refreshingly light and delightfully different.

    4 cups chicken stock
    1 cup finely chopped raw potato
    ½ cup finely chopped walnuts
    ½ cup cream
    salt and pepper

Heat stock to boiling, add potato and simmer 25 minutes. Add nuts and simmer another 10 minutes. Remove from heat, add cream and salt and pepper to taste. Serve immediately.
Serves 6.

FRENCH TERMS AND SOUPS

Je vis de bonne soupe et non de langage.
(I live on good soup, not on words.)
Moliere, *Les Femmes Savantes*

French terms used in cookbooks written in English can be very confusing to the layman, and I suspect they are often used for snobbish reasons. I have used only those French terms which are so familiar that they read like English anyway, and those which are difficult to translate briefly into English. *Purée*, *consommé* and *roux* belong to the first category, and three examples from the second category are: *beurre manie* (a smooth mixture of butter and flour used for thickening), *bouquet garni* (a mixture of aromatic herbs, the classics being parsley, thyme and bay leaf), and *julienne* (meaning cut into fine shreds like matchsticks, besides being the name of a consommé to which finely shredded vegetables are added).

Most of the soups in this book are named in English, even though many of them are French inspired. The influence is inevitable, since French is one of the world's three major cuisines and soups feature very heavily in French cooking. Nevertheless, a large number of French soups are named simply for their ingredients; *Potage aux huitres*, for instance, is oyster soup. A number of others have names which do not refer to their ingredients, but which have one major component, such as *Potage Crecy*, which is carrot soup. Soup names of both those types have been translated into English for this book.

There is a third category, however, which includes soups having a quite complex composition, and whose name in French fails to convey the ingredients. For these soups, I have kept the French titles, such as Bouillabaisse, Pot-au-feu and Vichyssoise.

Finally, to help those who have come across the French name of a soup and cannot find it in a reference book, here is a small glossary of common French soups which fall into the puzzling third category. You will find, by looking under the ingredients in the appropriate chapter, that a version of most of the following soups appears in this book.

Soupe Aigo Bouido — garlic soup.

Potage Ambassadeurs — fresh pea and sorrel soup.

Potage Bonne Femme — leek and potato soup.

Bourride — Provencal fish soup.

Potage Crecy — cream of carrot soup.

Potage Dubarry — cream of cauliflower soup.

Garbure — bean soup with vegetables.

Potage Germiny — cream of sorrel soup.

Matelote — freshwater fish soup with wine.

Panage — vegetable and bread soup.

Potage Parmentier — cream of leek and potato soup.

Potage Paysanne — mixed vegetable soup.

Potage Printanier — spring vegetable soup.

Soupe Purée a la Reine — purée of chicken soup.

Soupe Purée Saint-Germain — purée of fresh pea soup.

HERBS AND SPICES

What signifies knowing the Names, if you know not the Nature of Things?
Poor Richard's Almanack

Soups, like every other dish, can only be improved by the judicious addition of a herb or spice or two. Most recipes in this book have herbs and spices included, but if you wish to adventure or (and I suppose we all do some time or other) open a can or packet, then add a suitable herb or spice or extra meat or vegetables or a slurp of wine. It's marvellous just how simply you can make a common soup into something rather special. Use fresh herbs wherever possible and keep dried herbs and spices in airtight, preferably opaque, containers, away from the light. This helps keep them fresh and keep their colour. Using herbs and spices does inject personality into cooking and with trial and error and the following guide, you will improve the flavours of your soups.

This is not a glossary of all the herbs and spices from here to Zanzibar but simply a brief guide showing which common — and uncommon — herbs and spices will enhance which soups.

Allspice

Also known as Pimento or Jamaican Pepper, is not to be confused with Pimiento which is a member of the capsicum family. A native to the West Indies, allspice is pungent and sharply aromatic — a flavour of a mixture of spices — and is available commercially both whole and ground. In soups it is invariably used ground. Oxtail soup, beef and most meat soups gain value from a little allspice. Add it to tomato or vegetable soups. Try it too in Minestrone. It can be used as a garnish for all these soups.

Anise

This herb produces aniseed and is one of the sweetest smelling of herbs. It is a popular flavouring throughout Europe, is a member of the carrot family and is often used in fish soups and Bouillabaisse.

Basil

This is one of the finest, most delicate and fragrant of herbs. Sweet basil is most known for its affinity with tomatoes but goes well in other soups too. Basil can be added to beef or game soups, vegetable soups and chowders, Minestrone or pea soup. Shredded fresh basil garnishes many chilled vegetable soups perfectly. In Italy basil symbolises love.

Bay Leaves

Also known as laurel leaves, bay leaves come from the tree *Laurus nobilis* and grow in most temperate climates. Their mildly pungent flavour is a must in a bouquet garni for all soup stocks. They are marvellous as a flavouring for dried bean soups, for clear soups, in beef and vegetable soups, in pea soup and in chicken broths.

Caraway Seeds

The brown seeds of the caraway plant, which is of the parsley family and a native to Europe. Known to all in rye bread, caraway seeds are usually used whole but can be ground. Caraway Cream soup is said to stimulate the appetite of the sick. Caraway can be used in many vegetable soups, especially beetroot, cabbage and potato, in Chilli con Carne and in Goulash soup.

Cardamom

Only the dried ripe seeds of the cardamom plant are used and they are decidedly aromatic. Used ground, cardamom adds flavour to green pea soup and to many fruit soups.

Cayenne Pepper

Cayenne is a powder ground from the seeds and pods of various hot peppers originally grown in the Cayenne district of Africa. The taste is very pungent and hot and must be used sparingly. It adds zest and piquancy to meat soups and accents the natural flavours of such soups.

Celery Seed

These are the brown seeds of the vegetable celery. They have a characteristic celery aroma and add wonderful flavour to meat and vegetable soups, to fish soups and shellfish chowders. By and large celery seed can be used in any soup calling for fresh celery as a flavouring.

Chervil

A fine spring herb, chervil belongs to the parsley family. It symbolises sincerity and can be used in many delicate soups, especially chicken soups. Fresh chervil makes an excellent soup garnish in place of the ubiquitous parsley.

Chilli Powder

This is a blend of ground chillies, oregano, caraway seed, cumin and/or other spices. Fiery and hot, it is of course a must in Chilli con Carne but can be added to meat soups, dried bean soups or pea soup, not only as a background but to bring out flavours.

Chives

Chives are the most delicate member of the onion family. Chopped chives as a soup garnish are legend and if not available, chopped spring onion tops can be substituted. Their flavour is so delicate they are not really suitable for cooking in a soup.

Cinnamon

This reddish-brown curled bark of the evergreen cinnamon tree originated in Ceylon and the Malabar Coast of India. It is one of the oldest spices known to man and has a sweet, warm, aromatic and pungent taste. It is used either ground or in sticks or quills. Cinnamon is a must in cold fruit soups. It can be used in some meat soups too.

Cloves

The clove is one of the most fragrant of all spices. It is the unopened flower bud of an evergreen tree native to the Spice Islands (Indonesia). It resembles a little brown nail and is used either whole or ground. It is used in many fruit soups, in tomato soup and many other vegetable soups as well as meat soups. It gives excellent flavour to chicken stock too.

Coriander

Probably a native of Central Asia, the seeds are yellow-brown with a fragrantly pleasant scent. They are used mainly ground and go well in pea soup and artichoke soup. Chopped leaves of fresh coriander are excellent used instead of parsley as a soup garnish. It is also known as Chinese parsley or cilantro.

Cumin

Cumin has a strong scent and is warm, pungent and aromatic. It is an essential ingredient of curry powder for curried soups and goes well in many meat soups. It also adds a pleasant aroma to pea soup, lentil soup, potato soup, pumpkin soup and carrot soup.

Curry Powder

Curry powder is a blend of spices originally devised to preserve food in hot countries and not to disguise the elderly age of food as is often believed. It is an essential flavour in such soups as Mulligatawny and Senegalese soup as well as curry soups and some fruit soups.

Dill

Dill produces a leaf and a seed both of which are useful in soups. Dill leaves are feathery and fernlike and when chopped have an affinity for soups with sour cream and yoghurt or tomato and cucumber soups. Dill is excellent in most fish and shellfish soups and in chicken soups where either the leaves or seeds are used. The leaves, if used too freely, will impart a slightly bitter taste. Use dill too in pea soup and pumpkin soup.

Fennel

Almost all of the fennel plant is edible, including the seeds, leaves, stalks and bulbs. The fennel growing on the roadside is the common fennel, which is very pungent. The snipped leaves can however be used in fish soups. Florentine fennel or finocchio has a characteristic white bulb which makes an excellent soup itself. Fennel is good in most vegetable soups and general herb soups.

Garlic

Garlic is prized and disdained in just about equal measure. However, thank God, it is here to stay and a hint, a little or a mass of garlic will enhance nearly every soup. Remember that garlic tastes quite differently depending on whether it is whole, sliced, chopped or crushed. What more can be said?

Ginger

Both fresh (root or green) and ground ginger are used in cooking. Ginger is the root-tuber of an herbaceous plant of the ginger family. Coveted in Chinese cuisine, it features a lot in Chinese soups and goes well in some vegetable soups like tomato soup and pumpkin soup.

Juniper Berries

Not actually berries, but pea-sized dried, purplish-black cones of an evergreen tree of the pine family. Their taste is strong and they should be used sparingly. If you drink gin you will know the taste of juniper. A crushed berry or two work wonders in fruit soups, in tomato soup and in game soups.

Mace

Mace is the outer coating of the nutmeg and the taste is somewhat similar though milder. It goes well in tomato soups and fish soups.

Marjoram

Marjoram is an aromatic herb and belongs to the mint family. Its name derives from two Greek words meaning 'joy of the mountain'. It is mostly used dried and sparingly, as it is a pungent herb. It can be added to vegetable soups, especially mushroom, onion, tomato, spinach and pea soup. It is good in shellfish chowders and fish soups.

Mint

Along with parsley, this is a very widely used herb. There are many varieties of mint, the more popular being spearmint, applemint, eau-de-cologne and peppermint. They all have the same basic fresh flavour. Mint is excellent in pea soup and in cucumber or potato soup and can be used as a garnish for many chilled soups and some fruit soups.

Mustard

Whole yellow or brown mustard seeds are used or else the yellow seeds are used as mustard powder. The brown seeds are far more pungent than the yellow seeds and are usually only used in preparing varieties of table mustards. The yellow seeds can be added to mixed vegetable soups. Powdered mustard is good for some fish soups.

Nutmeg

Everyone is familiar with nutmeg. It is one of the slyest, and if used in a gingerly fashion, most seductive of flavours. There is no question that freshly grated nutmeg is far superior to the commercially ground variety. Nutmeg will enhance almost all soups, especially cream soups of vegetables, fish, chicken and game.

Oregano

Also spelt origanum and oreganum, it is frequently called wild marjoram, but is not nearly as strongly flavoured as marjoram. It is indispensable in Italian, Spanish, Mexican and Greek kitchens. Use it in tomato soup, vegetable soup, Minestrone and bean soups. It is also good in meat soups.

Paprika

This is the dried, ground powder of a sweet red pepper of the capsicum family. Its bright red, rich colour is ideal for garnishing colourless soups and its mildly pungent flavour is essential in Hungarian Goulash soup. Keep paprika in an opaque container otherwise the light will destroy its vibrant colour.

Parsley

The grandfather herb of the kitchen, parsley is used by nearly every cook in the world. As well as an excellent garnish, it is an essential ingredient of the bouquet garni. It is used as a flavouring in many soups and makes a beautiful soup on its own or mixed with vegetables. There are basically two sorts of parsley, the usual curly variety and the flat leaf type which is also called Italian parsley and is milder.

Rosemary

Rosemary is one of the most fragrant of herbs and has many unexpected uses. Like most herbs it is best used fresh but can be dried if necessary. It is excellent in meat soups, some chicken soups, in Minestrone, in spinach soup, in fish soups and for flavouring stocks.

Salad Burnett

A cool, refreshing herb, delicately tasting of cucumber. Float the leaves on top of hot or cold cream soups or cook them in hot soups, especially asparagus, mushroom, chicken and celery soups.

Saffron

Saffron is the dried, reddish-brown stigma of a flower of the crocus family. It is very expensive and has an aromatic and slightly bitter taste. It is used also for colouring as well as flavouring. It is good in fish soups, a must in Bouillabaisse and goes well in most meat soups and in chicken soup. Indian saffron or turmeric is a considerably lower-priced substitute for saffron.

Sage

A greyish-green herb that is another important culinary herb. Its aromatic, pungent, slightly bitter taste makes it a valuable addition to poultry soups, port and veal soups, fish soups and tomato or vegetable soups.

Savory

A mild herb of the mint family, savory has a slightly pungent camphor taste, whether of the summer or winter variety. It is good in potato soup, pea, bean or lentil soups and in mixed vegetable soups.

Sesame Seed

This is the creamy-white hulled seed of a herb of the sesamum family. Its taste is similar to toasted almonds. The seeds, toasted or not, can be used in bouillon or sprinkled on most thick soups as a garnish. Sesame oil is used in many Chinese soups.

Tarragon

The seductive flavour of French tarragon is far better when fresh rather than dried. It is excellent in many vegetable soups, mainly tomato, pea, mushroom and asparagus. It goes well in chicken soups too. Tarragon also makes an excellent soup on its own.

Thyme

Generally thyme is used sparingly as a background flavour but it can be laid heavily into onion soup. There are very few meat or vegetable or fish soups that do not benefit from the addition of thyme, even if it is only part of the bouquet garni.

Turmeric

Also known as Indian Saffron, turmeric is a substitute for true saffron. It is a golden-yellow powder ground from the dried root of an herbaceous plant. The root is similar to ginger. The taste is slightly bitter and aromatic. Turmeric is the yellow colouring of curry powder. Use it in soups instead of saffron.

Vanilla

This is the cured, dried bean of a creeper of the orchid family. It is also available as a liquid extract. The vanilla bean is used in many fruit soups.

SOUP GARNISHES

That's the ticket for soup.
London street saying

Topping off your soup with a suitably different garnish can change the whole temper of your meal. A garnish can add not only attraction but also flavour and texture. It can simply be a scattering of chopped parsley, or it can operate as in the days of French haute cuisine, when it could be more important than the dish itself, the garnish often having a grander name than the food under it.

Imagine a Vichyssoise or similar off-white soup without a garnish. In such cases a sprinkling of paprika and some chopped chives make all the difference. In most recipes an appropriate garnish is given, and it is worth remembering besides that there are many green herbs: watercress, chervil, coriander, chives, spring onion tops or cress can all replace parsley as a garnish. Try floating a small nasturtium flower and leaf on a cream soup.

Remember that lemons make excellent garnishes for many soups. A notched slice, a twist of peel, a few thin strips of lemon peel, a slice trimmed into a flower or lemon peel cut into tiny flowers, all look most attractive.

Even flowers, such as calendula petals or geranium petals, lend attraction to pale cream soups.

Strengthen the colour of a prawn bisque with a whole prawn perched on the side of the dish and an avocado slice floating nearby.

On a spinach or green soup, float tiny raw mushroom caps filled with sour cream and a few sprigs of a fresh green herb. Carved carrot flowers with chive stems look good on cream soups too.

Let your imagination run riot and to help it here is a list of ideas for garnishes for all soups. Just check that the garnish is compatible with the soup in colour, flavour and texture.

For light or clear soups

Finely chopped herbs — parsley, chives or spring onion tops, celery leaves, watercress, mint, onion, basil or chervil.
Thin slices of orange, lemon or lime.
A dab or swirl of whipped cream or sour cream sprinkled with chopped herbs and paprika.
Paprika.
A few sugar peas.
Bean sprouts.
Thin slices of cooked root vegetables (turnip or carrot) and chopped parsley.
Yoghurt.

For cream soups

Whipped cream or sour cream and a dusting of finely chopped fresh herbs.
Toasted shredded almonds or cashews.
Use the main ingredient — a sprig or some finely chopped green vegetable, slivers of ham, chicken, or seafood.
Corn chips.
Potato crisps.
Chopped and fried ham or bacon.
Paprika or strips of red or green peppers.

For thick soups

Many thick soups have enough colour to match their texture, many do not.
Thin slices of orange, lemon or lime.
Sliced hard-boiled eggs.
Croutons.
Sour cream or whipped cream.
Grated cheeses.
Sliced cooked sausage, frankfurters or small salami-type sausages.
Dumplings.

SOUP ACCOMPANIMENTS

You can't get into the soup in Ireland, do what you like.

Evelyn Waugh, *Decline and Fall*

When you have selected the soup to precede the meal or as the meal itself, there is another decision: whether to serve an accompaniment, and if so, what. Basically this will depend on the style of the soup or meal. First, a light soup before a large dinner will not usually require an accompaniment. Bulk will follow in later courses, but in some cases paper-thin melba toast, wafery cracker biscuits or a few croutons could be included to give the light soup texture. With fairly filling soups, crackers, light breads, garlic toast, bread sticks, cheese puffs or thins, etc. could be served on the side. And for main course soups, an accompaniment will always be necessary: dumplings, scones, muffins, rolls, a host of breads and biscuits. There are all sorts of crackers available: water crackers, wheaten biscuits, table thins, flavoured biscuits. And as for breads, these range from the bland, American-style, candy-floss white, sliced bread through to wonderful wholewheat, dark, super-tasting continental style breads. Always remember to keep the accompaniments the same style as the soup: for a light soup, a dainty accompaniment; for a heavy soup, a hearty accompaniment.

Breads to serve as side dishes

French bread.
A selection of the myriads of plaits and twists, cobs and different shapes of rye and brown breads.
Small white rolls.
A selection from the many rye, brown and wholewheat rolls.
Bread sticks.
Plain crackers with or without a spread of herb butter, cheese spreads or fish paste.
Corn bread or corn pone.
Cheese wafers, thins, puffs, etc.
Small choux pastry puffs.
Croutons, plain, with garlic or herbs.
Melba toast.
Toasted bread cut into different or fancy shapes.
Lebanese (Pita) bread.

Cheese Thins

1 cup plain flour
½ teaspoon salt
¼ teaspoon paprika
pinch cayenne
¾ cup grated tasty cheddar cheese
2 tablespoons grated parmesan cheese
¼ cup cold beer
1 egg yolk
2 tablespoons beer for wash
caraway or poppy seeds

In a bowl combine the flour, salt, paprika and cayenne. Add the cheddar cheese and parmesan cheese and blend the mixture well. Add the cold beer, toss the mixture until the beer is incorporated and form the dough into a cylinder about 2.5 cm in diameter. Wrap the dough in foil and freeze for at least an hour. Slice the dough in 3–4 cm thick rounds and arrange them on baking trays about 2.5 cm apart. Brush the rounds with an egg wash made by beating the egg yolk with 2 tablespoons beer. Sprinkle them with caraway or poppy seeds.

Bake in a pre-heated, very hot oven, 230°C, for 12 to 14 minutes until the thins are slightly coloured.

Makes about 36 cheese thins.

Cheese Puffs

1 cup grated tasty cheese
¾ cup flour
2 teaspoons baking powder
pinch cayenne pepper
pinch salt
chopped chives
1 egg beaten into 2 tablespoons milk

Mix the egg and milk into the dry ingredients. Spoon into greased patty tins and bake in 200°C oven for 10 minutes. Best eaten while still warm, with or without butter.

Cheese Wafers

1¼ cups flour
125 g butter, grated
150 g tasty cheese, grated
½ teaspoon baking powder
½ teaspoon cayenne pepper

Mix all ingredients together and knead until mixture holds together. Make into a long roll. Wrap in greaseproof paper and chill in refrigerator for about 3 hours. Slice the roll in thin rounds and bake in moderate oven for 20 minutes or until golden and crisp. When cooled a little carefully slide them off the tray.

One-Knead White Bread Rolls

The shops in our neck of the woods are full of all sorts of delicious brown, wholemeal, wholewheat breads and bread rolls and white, French, German, Irish and Lebanese breads, etc. But it is almost impossible to get really nice fresh white rolls. So here is an excellent recipe for white rolls. It is less time-consuming than most and goes well with most soups. You should have an inkling of bread making before you tackle them however.

2 heaped dessertspoons flour
2 heaped dessertspoons sugar
2 level dessertspoons active dry yeast
1 cup warm water

Mix all the ingredients well and leave the 'sponge' until it begins to work well, about half an hour.

5 cups flour
1½ teaspoons salt
1 knob butter
water/milk

Add the above to the 'sponge' and enough water/milk mixture — about 1¾ cups — to make a wet dough, just stirring, not kneading. Put in a warm place and cover with a tea towel to prevent drying out. Allow to rise to double in size. Scrape the dough out of the bowl onto a well-floured board and gradually add about ¼ cup flour as you knead to make a smooth, elastic and shiny dough. Knead for about 10 minutes, not too heavily.

This can then be put into 2 x 500 g greased loaf tins or, since we want rolls, flatten out the dough, cut into small rounds with a biscuit cutter, roll into balls and place on greased oven trays, not too close together. Put in a warm place and allow to rise to double in size. Bake in a pre-heated 180°C oven for about ¾ hour or until the rolls are golden and crisp. Open one to test.

If you are making bread, bake for about an hour or until the bread sounds hollow when it is tapped.

And note that bread sticks, oval rolls, long rolls, twists, plaits and crescent rolls can all be made from this dough. If you wish, before baking, the rolls can be brushed with egg/milk mixture and dusted with sesame seeds or poppy seeds.

Corn Bread

1 cup plain flour
1 cup fine cornmeal
3 teaspoons baking powder
½ teaspoon salt
1 cup milk
1 egg
¼ cup vegetable oil

Mix all dry ingredients together. Beat egg, oil and milk together and pour into dry mixture. Pour into greased 22.5 cm pan and bake in pre-heated oven at 200°C for about 25–30 minutes. Test centre of bread with knife to be sure it is thoroughly cooked.

Serves 4–6.

Fried Croutons

Plain
Take a fairly thick slice of stale bread (wholewheat bread makes interesting croutons), remove the crust and cut it into small or medium dice.

In a frying pan, heat a mixture of butter and oil and carefully fry the croutons on both sides until golden brown. Take care not to burn. Use immediately or allow to cool and store in an airtight jar and reheat before using, and add to the soup bowls at the last minute.

With Garlic
Fry some sliced garlic in the butter and oil until golden, then remove the garlic and add the bread cubes and proceed as before.

With Herbs
Lightly fry some finely chopped fresh herbs (parsley, thyme, basil, tarragon, etc.) in the butter and oil for a minute or so, then add the bread cubes and proceed as before.

With Cheese
Make plain croutons, and while they are still hot, sprinkle generously with parmesan cheese, making sure the croutons are well coated.

Corn Spoon

3 eggs, separated
1½ cups scalded milk
¾ cup fine cornmeal
¾ teaspoon salt
2 tablespoons butter
450 g can cream-style sweet corn
¾ teaspoon baking powder

Grease a 4½ litre casserole dish. Beat the egg yolks until thick and lemon coloured. Beat the egg whites until stiff but not dry. In a saucepan stir cornmeal and salt into scalded milk, beating hard. Cook a few seconds over low heat, stirring until it is the consistency of thick mush. Blend in the butter and sweet corn, then baking powder. Fold in the egg yolks, then the egg whites.

Pour into baking dish. Bake 190°C for about 35 minutes or until it is puffy and golden brown, and a knife inserted in centre comes out clean.

Serves 4–6.

Herb Dumplings

Good on any hearty, meaty soup.

1 cup flour
pinch salt
1 tablespoon finely chopped suet
1 teaspoon finely chopped parsley
½ teaspoon finely chopped tarragon or thyme
a little finely chopped onion
½ teaspoon baking powder
water

Mix the dry ingredients together. Add enough cold water to make dough stick together, adding very little at a time, stirring quickly with a knife. Knead into a ball. Turn out onto a floured board. Cut into 12 portions. Roll into small balls and put on top of soup half an hour before serving.

Serves 6.

Cheddar Cheese Dumplings

Great with any beef-based soup.

Place 1 cup self-raising flour, salt and pepper, ⅓ cup shredded suet, ⅓ cup finely grated cheddar cheese in a bowl. Mix in enough water to make a slack dough. Divide into eight portions and place these on top of the simmering soup. Cover saucepan and cook 15 to 20 minutes.
Serves 8.

Scones

  3 cups self-raising flour
  3 teaspoons baking powder
  ¼ teaspoon salt
  2 tablespoons butter
  about 1 cup milk and water mixed

Sift the dry ingredients, rub in the butter and mix to soft dough with the milk/water mixture. Knead lightly on a floured board, roll out, cut into rounds, put on a cold oven tray, and bake for 10 minutes at 220°C.

Cheese Scones

  3 cups self-raising flour
  3 teaspoons baking powder
  ½ teaspoon salt
  pinch cayenne pepper
  1 cup grated tasty cheese
  about 1 cup milk and water mixed

Sift the dry ingredients, add the cheese and mix to a light dough with the milk and water. Turn onto a floured board, knead lightly, roll out fairly thickly and cut into desired shapes. Place on a cold tray and bake 10 minutes at 220°C.

Bacon Muffins

butter
6 rashers bacon
2 cups sifted flour
2 teaspoons baking powder
2 tablespoons sugar
¾ teaspoon salt
1 egg, beaten
1 cup milk
2 tablespoons bacon fat

Butter 15 muffin cups and pre-heat oven to 200°C. Fry the bacon until crisp, drain it, reserving the fat, and chop it. Sift together the flour, baking powder, sugar and salt. Mix the egg, milk and bacon fat. Add to dry ingredients along with the bacon and stir only until the flour is dampened. Mixture will look somewhat lumpy but do not beat. Fill the muffin cups ⅔ full and bake about 25 minutes.

Paper-Thin Melba Toast

Toast sliced white bread, then remove the crusts. Place the toast on a flat board and with a sharp knife split each slice in two (you will be surprised how easy this is). Put into a baking tray and dry out in a slow oven. Store in an airtight container or plastic bag until ready to use.

Garlic Toast

Peel a large clove of garlic and cut it in half. Make toast in the usual way. While the toast is still hot rub the cut side of the garlic into the toast. The more you rub, the more garlic melts into the toast and the stronger the flavour. Butter the toast and serve it immediately.

Index

Digby Law's

PICKLE & CHUTNEY
COOKBOOK

A New Zealand classic

Digby Law's Pickle & Chutney Cookbook is a New Zealand classic used and respected by home cooks and professionals alike. This indispensable reference contains 300 easy-to-make recipes for chutneys, relishes, sauces, oils, pickles, jellies, vinegars and mustards. Discover traditional preserves from Europe and North America, exotic specialties from Asia and Latin America, and enjoy familiar New Zealand favourites. Now back in print for the first time in almost 10 years, this classic deserves a place in every New Zealand kitchen.

Digby Law's

VEGETABLE
COOKBOOK

A New Zealand classic

When this book was first published in 1978 it became an instant classic; it has been reprinted over 16 times and is still recognised as one of the best vegetable recipe collections available. It provides over 400 superb recipes that make the most of the combinations, flavours and textures of delicious fresh New Zealand produce. Recipes include side dishes, salads, mains, desserts, dressings and sauces. *Digby Law's Vegetable Cookbook* has clear and simple instructions, an emphasis on using only the very best ingredients, and the imagination and flair that the author brings to all his cooking. Now back in print by popular demand, this classic deserves a place in every New Zealand kitchen.